The Beatles

BY JOHN ROBERTSON

Copyright © 1994 Omnibus Press (A Division of Book Sales Limited)

Edited by Chris Charlesworth
Cover & Book designed by 4i Limited
Picture research by David Brolan

ISBN: 0.7119.3548.3 Order No: OP 47368

Exclusive Distributors
Book Sales Limited, 8/9 Frith Street, London W1V 5TZ, UK.
Music Sales Corporation, 257 Park Avenue South, New York, NY 10010, USA.
Music Sales Pty Limited, 120 Rothschild Avenue, Rosebery, NSW 2018, Australia.

To the Music Trade only:
Music Sales Limited, 8/9, Frith Street, London W1V 5TZ, UK.

Photo credits:
All photographs supplied by London Features International: Pictorial Press: Redferns.

Every effort has been made to trace the copyright holders of the photographs in this book but one or two were unreachable. We would be grateful if the photographers concerned would contact us.

Printed in the United Kingdom by Stanley L. Hunt Butler & Son Limited, Worcester.

A catalogue record for this book is available from the British Library.

OMNIBUS PRESS
LONDON · NEW YORK · SYDNEY

Contents

INTRODUCTION v

The Albums

    PLEASE PLEASE ME 1

    WITH THE BEATLES 9

    A HARD DAY'S NIGHT 17

    BEATLES FOR SALE 25

    HELP! 33

    RUBBER SOUL 41

    REVOLVER 49

    SERGEANT PEPPER'S LONELY HEARTS CLUB BAND 57

    MAGICAL MYSTERY TOUR 65

    THE BEATLES: THE WHITE ALBUM 73

    YELLOW SUBMARINE 87

    ABBEY ROAD 91

    LET IT BE 101

    PAST MASTERS VOLUME I 109

    PAST MASTERS VOLUME II 117

    THE BEATLES 1962-1966 THE RED ALBUM 127

    THE BEATLES 1967-1970 THE BLUE ALBUM 127

Non EMI sessions

    THE TONY SHERIDAN SESSIONS 129

    THE DECCA AUDITION 131

    LIVE AT THE STAR CLUB, HAMBURG 133

TRACK LISTING 137

Introduction

The Beatles revolutionised pop music in the Sixties. A cliché? Yes, of course. But it's become a cliché simply because it's true, and because a cliché is the only possible response to something as overwhelming and staggering as The Beatles' career.

In the artificially-hyped multinational media world of the 1990s, The Beatles' sales figures will be, and are being, outclassed by entertainers with barely a fraction of their talent and artistry. But those achievements wouldn't have been possible without The Beatles, who rescued a brand of popular music that was in danger of fading into oblivion, and turned it into a medium that produced million-dollar returns – and art. That, finally, is The Beatles' greatest claim to fame. Working under immense pressure, to schedules that would baffle the sedentary superstars of the modern era, they produced thirteen great albums, and more than 20 singles, in a little over seven years.

Not only that, they never ceased to stretch and broaden the palette of pop and rock – incorporating the lyrical poetry of folk singers like Bob Dylan, the psychedelia of the American West Coast, the jangle of folk-rock and the gutsiness of roots genres like blues and country, without sounding for a second like anyone but themselves. Masters of pastiche, they were also the most original and experimental artists in rock history – eager always to push at boundaries, to find out what might happen if you played that instrument in that room with the tape running backwards and all pre-conceptions left outside the door.

Incorporating influences from every branch of popular music, and even beyond to the classical world, they returned the compliment in full, inspiring musicians in rock, pop, folk, jazz, R&B, country and blues in a way that will never be possible in the future. Their fashions, argot and habits were imitated by millions. They set the social agenda for the West's most playful and adventurous decade of this century. They provided the soundtrack for a generation. And they also taped about 200 of the greatest pop records of all time, examined in the following pages, CD album-by-album.

Few artists in any field affect a generation beyond their own. To survive more than 20 or 30 years after your death requires a combination of genius and luck. After that, it's in the lap of the gods. But alone of the pop performers of the 20th Century, it's safe to predict that The Beatles' music will live forever.

Please Please Me

PARLOPHONE

CDP7 46435 2

It requires a leap of the imagination to return to the innocent days of 1963, when The Beatles recorded and released their first two long-playing albums. The common currency of teenage pop was the three-minute single, or at a stretch the two-for-the-price-of-two 45rpm extended player (EP). Albums, or LPs as they were universally known in the early Sixties, were regarded as being beyond the financial reach of most teenagers; and with the oldest of The Beatles themselves no more than 22 when their first album was recorded, the teen audience was definitely EMI's target. Only adult performers like Frank Sinatra and Ella Fitzgerald were allowed to use the 30- or 40-minute expanse of the LP as a personal artistic statement. For the rest, the LP was unashamedly a cash-in – either for a film, or else for die-hard supporters entranced by a hit single or two. Hence the full title of The Beatles' début album, which defined its selling points precisely: 'Please Please Me, Love Me Do and 12 other songs'.

Much has been made of the fact that 10 of the record's 14 tracks were recorded during one day; but that was the way the pop business operated in 1963. This haste was proof of The Beatles' junior status at EMI, and also of the company's desire to rush an LP onto the market before teenage Britain found a new set of heroes. Remember that the band had yet to score their first No. 1 when the album was recorded: the extended session represented a commendable act of faith on the behalf of producer George Martin.

Four of the album's titles were already in the can, via their first two singles, 'Love Me Do' and 'Please Please Me'. The rest – a mix of originals and covers – was a cross-section of their typical concert fare, with one exception: the group's penchant for covers of Chuck Berry and Little Richard rock'n'rollers was ignored, presumably because George Martin believed the era of rock'n'roll was past.

Recorded on two-track at Abbey Road, the album was mixed into mono and very rudimentary stereo – the latter format claiming only a tiny proportion of the market in 1963. Until 1968, The Beatles regarded the mono versions of their albums as the authentic representation of their work; and if they'd been asked, they would no doubt have agreed with George Martin's decision to prepare the CD mix of 'Please Please Me' in mono. But stereophiles, particularly in America, regarded this decision as barbarism in disguise, and continue to lobby for the release of the CD in stereo.

I SAW HER STANDING THERE
JOHN LENNON/PAUL McCARTNEY
RECORDED 11 FEBRUARY 1963

With a simple count-in, Paul McCartney captured all The Beatles' youthful exuberance in the opening seconds of their début album. Lyrically naïve, melodically unpolished, 'I Saw Her Standing There' was still classic Beatles' rock'n'roll – Lennon and McCartney trading

vocals as if they were chewing gum between syllables, the falsetto 'ooos' that soon became a Beatles trademark, the rising chords of the middle eight that promised some kind of sexual climax, and the tight-but-loose vigour of the playing. And the record ended with a triumphant clang of a guitar chord matched by a whoop from McCartney. No doubt about it, The Beatles had arrived.

MISERY
JOHN LENNON/PAUL McCARTNEY
RECORDED 11, 20 FEBRUARY 1963

Right from the start of their recording career, The Beatles were encouraged by manager Brian Epstein to work as a songwriting factory, turning out hits to order for other artists. By February 1963, their reputation had yet to acquire its later power, and fellow performers more often than not turned them down. Helen Shapiro was offered this Lennon composition the week before The Beatles recorded it themselves, but her management declined. Unabashed, Lennon and McCartney romped through what was supposed to be a declaration of lovelorn anguish like two schoolboys on half-day holiday. Never has a song about misery sounded so damn cheerful.

Trivia note: the sheet music for this song, as copied by Kenny Lynch's early cover version, gives the first line as: "You've been treating me bad, misery." Lennon and McCartney sang something much more universal: "The world's been treating me bad".

ANNA (GO TO HIM)
ARTHUR ALEXANDER
RECORDED 11 FEBRUARY 1963

If The Beatles had been allowed more than a day to make this album, they would no doubt have re-recorded the instrumental backing for this rather laboured cover of an Arthur Alexander R&B hit. But there was no faulting Lennon's vocal, which had already hit upon the mixture of romantic disillusionment and supreme self-interest that became his trademark when tackling a love song. It was almost sabotaged, though, by the pedestrian nature of McCartney and Harrison's backing vocals.

CHAINS
GERRY GOFFIN/CAROLE KING
RECORDED 11 FEBRUARY 1963

At The Beatles' Decca audition in January 1962, George Harrison threatened to surface as their prime lead vocalist. A year later, he'd already been relegated to cameo appearances, as on this charmingly cheerful cover of The Cookies' New York girl-group hit, which The Beatles had only recently added to their repertoire.

BOYS
LUTHER DIXON/WES FARRELL
RECORDED 11 FEBRUARY 1963

If George was restricted to cameos, Ringo Starr's vocal contributions to The Beatles' recording career were purely tokens, to keep his fans from causing a fuss. He bawled his way through The Shirelles' 1960 US hit with enthusiasm if not subtlety, nailing the song in just one take. Presumably nobody in 1963 stopped to wonder why Ringo was singing a lyric that lauded the joys of boys, rather than the opposite sex. The song had been a Beatles standard for a couple of years, Ringo having inherited the number from former drummer Pete Best.

ASK ME WHY
JOHN LENNON/PAUL McCARTNEY
RECORDED 26 NOVEMBER 1962

Unlike Paul McCartney, John Lennon took time to slide into the conventions of pop songwriting. 'Ask Me Why' illustrated what happened before he acquired the knack. From the difficult rhythm of the opening lines to the cut-and-paste structure of the middle section, it was a song that seemed to have been constructed painfully, bar-by-bar, rather than flowing naturally like McCartney's early efforts. Careful study of his role models, like Smokey Robinson and Arthur Alexander, soon rewarded Lennon with a keen grasp of the essentials of composing, though not in time to prevent this number being consigned to the flipside of 'Please Please Me'.

PLEASE PLEASE ME
JOHN LENNON/PAUL McCARTNEY
RECORDED 26 NOVEMBER 1962

Though no evidence remains on tape, The Beatles' original arrangement of 'Please Please Me' was apparently closer to a Roy Orbison ballad than a beat group number. It was attempted during the group's second EMI session in September 1962, George Martin remembering it as "a very dreary song". He suggested that the group soup up the arrangement – something that was done to such effect that it became their first No. 1 at the end of February 1963.

In up tempo form, it became an overt sexual invitation on Lennon's part, and a clear sign that The Beatles were more than just another pop group. Their harmonies, the opening harmonica riff, and Ringo's accomplished drumming testified to a remarkable surge in confidence since their first EMI sessions.

As with 'Love Me Do', there are two different versions of this song on EMI releases. The stereo mix, unavailable on CD, utilised an alternate take on which Lennon and McCartney messed up their vocals. Quite how that blatant a mistake escaped the notice of George Martin remains to be answered.

LOVE ME DO
JOHN LENNON/PAUL McCARTNEY
RECORDED 11 SEPTEMBER 1962

Despite the claim on the album cover, this track wasn't the one issued on the first Beatles single. It was the same song, true enough, but not the same recording. At the group's début session, on 4 September 1962, they had struggled through more than 15 takes of 'Love Me Do' before George Martin was remotely satisfied. A week later, they returned to London, to find session drummer Andy White ready to take Ringo Starr's place. Having only recently replaced Pete Best in the band, Ringo must have wondered whether his own days were numbered. White duly handled the sticks on a remake of the song, with Ringo dejectedly banging a tambourine on the sidelines.

For reasons that remain unclear, it was the initial version of 'Love Me Do' which appeared as the group's first 45. But when their album was assembled, George Martin elected to use the Andy White recording instead – presumably because the tape of the single had been sent overseas to an EMI subsidiary. Later in 1963, the decision was made to use the White take on all future pressings of the single, as well; and from then until 1982, Ringo's recording début with The Beatles remained officially unavailable.

The song itself was a genuine Lennon/McCartney collaboration, its plodding beat enlivened by Lennon's harmonica solo. That was a gimmick he picked up from Bruce Channel's spring 1962 hit, 'Hey Baby', and proceeded to use many times over the next two years. Without the gimmick, 'Love Me Do' hadn't previously been regarded as one of the highlights of the group's original repertoire.

P.S. I LOVE YOU
JOHN LENNON/PAUL McCARTNEY
RECORDED 11 SEPTEMBER 1962

There's a clear division in The Beatles' early work between the songs they wrote before 'Please Please Me', and the ones that came immediately after. McCartney's 'P.S. I Love You' dated from the early months of 1962, and had the slightly forced feel of 'Love Me Do' and 'Ask Me Why' – with only Paul's swoop into the upper register for the last middle section to suggest that any great genius was on display. Like 'Ask Me Why', it qualified for the album solely because it had appeared on the flipside of a single.

BABY IT'S YOU
HAL DAVID/BURT BACHARACH
BARNEY WILLIAMS
RECORDED 11, 20 FEBRUARY 1963

Lennon may have sounded slightly ill-at-ease on his own songs, but with covers, he already had the confidence of a born interpreter. The group's boyish harmonies didn't distract him from giving another Shirelles hit a commanding vocal performance that marked him out as The Beatles' most distinctive voice.

DO YOU WANT TO KNOW A SECRET?
JOHN LENNON/PAUL McCARTNEY
RECORDED 11 FEBRUARY 1963

Given away simultaneously to fellow Brian Epstein protégé Billy J. Kramer (for a hit single), and to George Harrison (for this LP), 'Do You Want To Know A Secret?' was a Lennon composition — inspired by a line he

remembered from a Disney song that his mother used to sing. "I thought it would be a good vehicle for George because it only had three notes and he wasn't the best singer in the world," Lennon explained charitably in later years.

A TASTE OF HONEY
RIC MARLOW/BOBBY SCOTT
RECORDED 11 FEBRUARY 1963

In Hamburg and Liverpool, The Beatles were required to work up a sheaf of ballads and standards, which would melt the hearts of even the most anti-rock audience they would be forced to entertain. McCartney was the Beatle with the heritage in pre-Elvis pop, and it fell to him to perform the group's token demonstration of 'sophistication' – an American song recorded most notably by Lenny Welch, but fast becoming a favourite among sedate jazzmen and big bands around the world.

In retrospect, the inclusion of this song seems laughable – the Stones would never have made such a blatant cop-out – but in McCartney's capable hands, 'A Taste Of

Honey' became another slice of Beatle music. The group didn't much care for the song, though: when they performed it live, Lennon invariably changed the chorus to 'A Waste Of Money'.

THERE'S A PLACE
JOHN LENNON/PAUL McCARTNEY
RECORDED 11 FEBRUARY 1963

Forget the theory that John Lennon only started singing about himself when he started taking drugs. Listen to the words of this cheery beat tune, and you'll find his first piece of self-analysis: "There's a place where I can go, when I feel low, when I feel blue. And it's my mind, and there's no time when I'm alone." No-one – not even Bob Dylan – was writing songs like that in 1963. But nobody told John Lennon that. The result: the first self-conscious rock song, beating The Beach Boys' equally self-obsessed 'In My Room' by several months.

TWIST AND SHOUT
BERT RUSSELL/PHIL MEDLEY
RECORDED 11 FEBRUARY 1963

"I couldn't sing the damn thing, I was just screaming." So said John Lennon, about the first take of the final song recorded during The Beatles' marathon 11 February session. His voice shot by the rigours of the day's schedule, and unable to fall upon the twin crutches of pills and booze which had fuelled The Beatles on their night-long gigs in Hamburg, Lennon simply shredded his vocal cords in the interests of rock'n'roll.

Until McCartney matched it with 'Long Tall Sally' a year later, this was the supreme Beatles rocker – a cover, ironically enough, of a tune that The Isley Brothers had rescued from an abysmal original recording by Phil Spector's charges, The Top Notes. In that one take, Lennon cut Britain's best rock'n'roll record to date, and the band kept pace with him, right down to Ringo's exultant flourish on the drums as The Beatles reached home.

with
the
beatles

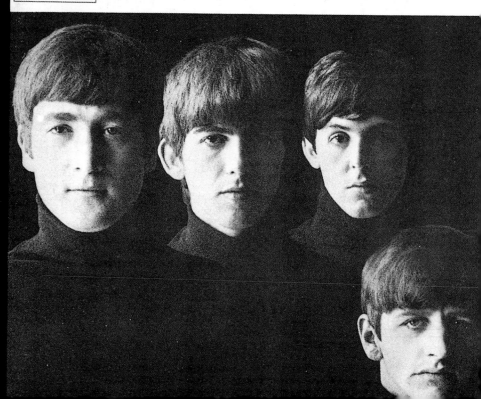

With The Beatles

PARLOPHONE

CDP7 46436 2

Four months after they released their début album, The Beatles began work on their follow-up. By the time it was released, in November 1963, the group were the hottest product in British show-business. Second time around, there was no need to sell the album on the reputation of a recent hit single: with Christmas on the horizon, EMI knew the fans would buy anything The Beatles released. What they didn't realise, though, was that 'With The Beatles' would prove to be such a giant step beyond their hastily assembled début.

The cover artwork immediately revealed that more thought had gone into this album than its predecessor. Whereas 'Please Please Me' used the standard smiling pop pose as its cover design, 'With The Beatles' boasted a much artier Robert Freeman photo, with the group's heads arranged in careful line, shot in half-light. It emerged later that this trick was simply borrowed from much earlier pictures of the group, taken by the German photographer Astrid Kirchherr. But as far as the public was concerned, the artwork was startlingly new.

Musically, too, 'With The Beatles' announced that the revolution had arrived. The Beatles kept faithfully to the same mix of originals and outside songs that had filled their first long-player, but they were already beginning to play the studio as an instrument. On 'Please Please Me', they'd briefly discovered the potential joys of overdubbing. Now, with more time on their hands, they went to town.

"The first set of tricks was double-tracking on the second album," John Lennon admitted many years later. "We were told we could do it, and that really set the ball rolling. We double-tracked ourselves off the second album." And they did it without sacrificing an ounce of the freshness and exuberance that had become The Beatles' hallmark – audible most clearly on the mono mix of the record, which was again favoured by George Martin for the CD release.

IT WON'T BE LONG
JOHN LENNON/PAUL McCARTNEY
RECORDED 30 JULY 1963

Throughout their career, The Beatles never lost sight of the importance of having hit singles. Certainly in 1963, their continued production of hits was their passport to the future, and they blatantly concocted potential chartbusters as and when required. Lennon and McCartney competed for the honour of winning an A-side, with only pride and prestige at stake – the songwriting royalties for all their songs were split equally between them, after all.

Like 'She Loves You', the single they recorded a month earlier, Lennon's 'It Won't Be Long' was built around a 'yeah, yeah' chorus. Two singles with the same gimmick would have become a straitjacket, so 'It Won't Be Long' was 'relegated' to the position of lead track on the album, where it was every bit as effective a hook as 'I Saw Her Standing There' had been on 'Please Please Me'.

ALL I'VE GOT TO DO
JOHN LENNON/PAUL McCARTNEY
RECORDED 11 SEPTEMBER 1963

Compare this song to 'Ask Me Why', written around a year earlier, and the rapid maturity in Lennon's songwriting is immediately apparent. John singled out Arthur Alexander (the man who'd written 'Anna', plus several other Beatles stage favourites) as his prime inspiration for this soulful ballad. He stretched the word 'I' over seven syllables in the opening line, using all the melismatic flair of Sam Cooke or Jackie Wilson, and proved how well he understood the power of melody by shifting into a higher register for the final chorus as a cry of passion. It was a remarkably assured performance, which would have been beyond anyone else in the group at this early stage of their career.

ALL MY LOVING
JOHN LENNON/PAUL McCARTNEY
RECORDED 30 JULY 1963

While Lennon was converting emotion into music, McCartney was writing unforgettable melodies. Classical students claim there's a tune of Tchaikovsky's buried in 'All My

Loving', but it's an irrelevant point, as the finished song is pure Beatles – the most commercial song they recorded in 1963 that wasn't issued as a single. Often maligned as musicians, The Beatles prove their worth on this song: Harrison's lead break is beautifully tidy and restrained, while Lennon's lightning rhythm guitar playing is the powerhouse of the arrangement.

DON'T BOTHER ME
GEORGE HARRISON
RECORDED 12 SEPTEMBER 1963

"That was the first song that I wrote, as an exercise to see if I could write a song," George Harrison confessed in his autobiography, *I Me Mine.* "I don't think it's particularly good." Faced by two prolific bandmates, Harrison was envious of their ability and their royalty cheques. Liverpool friend Bill Harry nagged George on the subject while he was ill in bed during a Beatles tour, and Harrison responded by turning his reaction into a slightly clumsy but reasonably accomplished song. Interestingly, it didn't sound anything like his own musical heroes, Carl Perkins or Goffin and King, but came out as a facsimile of what Lennon and McCartney were writing – just as beat groups across the country were doing in their bedrooms.

LITTLE CHILD
JOHN LENNON/PAUL McCARTNEY
RECORDED 12 SEPTEMBER, 3 OCTOBER 1963

Even The Beatles occasionally sounded like tired hacks, though this early in their career, they could always summon the enthusiasm to hide their lack of inspiration. Five years later, this contrived but chirpy pop tune would have been classed as bubblegum. But on 'With The Beatles', Lennon and McCartney's dynamic vocals and Lennon's chest-expanding harmonica solo turned a piece of hackwork into 106 seconds of pure energy.

TILL THERE WAS YOU
MEREDITH WILLSON
RECORDED 30 JULY 1963

Standards time again, as Paul filled the 'A Taste Of Honey' slot with the hit song from the Broadway musical, *The Music Man*. He sang the song as if he meant every word, and George Harrison contributed an accomplished acoustic guitar solo – so accomplished, in fact, that some cynics have questioned whether he actually played it. But the solo on the rendition they recorded onstage in Hamburg was equally dextrous, so unless they'd smuggled a session man into the Star Club, George was the man.

PLEASE MR. POSTMAN
DOBBIN/GARRETT/GARMAN/BRIANBERT
RECORDED 30 JULY 1963

During 1963, the American stable of Motown labels, owned by Berry Gordy, began to enjoy regular distribution for their youthful soul records in Britain. The Beatles were instant fans, to the extent that three of the tracks on 'With The Beatles' were covers of recent Motown hits.

On their first album, 'Chains' and 'Anna'

had been enthusiastic renditions of outside songs, without threatening to become definitive. On 'Twist And Shout', however, and again with The Marvelettes' 'Please Mr. Postman', Lennon's performance was so magical that it made the original sound like an imitation. The Beatles tightened up The Marvelettes' vocal arrangement, while Lennon's lead dripped with authority and self-confidence. It was a thrilling conclusion to the first side of the album, which had already seen the group tackling everything from soul to rock to balladry with ease.

ROLL OVER BEETHOVEN
CHUCK BERRY
RECORDED 30 JULY 1963

Even before there was a Beatles, Lennon, McCartney and Harrison had been performing this Chuck Berry rock'n'roll standard from 1956. During 1961, the song passed from John's hands to George, who also had to double as lead guitarist – fine in the studio, when he could overdub the solo, but prone to being more erratic onstage. Despite their heritage as a rock'n'roll band, The Beatles sounded

strangely uncomfortable the first time they cut an authentic American rock song in the studio, hurrying the pace to the point that George had problems fitting all the words into each line.

HOLD ME TIGHT
JOHN LENNON/PAUL McCARTNEY
RECORDED 12 SEPTEMBER 1963

During the sessions for their first album, The Beatles had taped and then abandoned a version of this self-composed beat number – and the tape was subsequently destroyed. If the take that *was* considered good enough for release is anything to go by, the original must have been disastrous, as this remake has a McCartney vocal that strays distressingly off key, to the point that neighbouring dogs are likely to howl with distress. Only a handful of Beatles recordings can be said to be below par, but this is one of them.

YOU REALLY GOT A HOLD ON ME
WILLIAM 'SMOKEY' ROBINSON
RECORDED 18 JULY 1963

Not so 'You Really Got A Hold On Me', Lennon's second brilliant hijacking of a Motown song. Sublime though The Miracles' original is, it's easily outclassed by The Beatles' effortless interpretation. John's vocal could be used as a dictionary definition of reluctant infatuation, while the decision to dramatise the phrase 'tied up' with a repeated break in the rhythm was a stroke of genius. The response vocals challenged George's limited range to the hilt, but sheer enthusiasm won the day, as The Beatles stole another American song for their own.

I WANNA BE YOUR MAN
JOHN LENNON/PAUL McCARTNEY
RECORDED 11, 12, 30 SEPTEMBER, 3, 23 OCTOBER 1963

By the time The Beatles finished work on this song, they knew that The Rolling Stones were issuing it as their second single. As the story goes, Stones manager Andrew Oldham spotted Lennon and McCartney in a London street, bundled them into his car, and requested a song for his new band. The Beatles played the Stones the chorus of 'I Wanna Be Your Man', then went into another office to finish the bridge – emerging an hour or so later to display the completed effort to their visibly impressed juniors. The Stones played the song as an R&B tune; The Beatles gave it to Ringo, whereupon it became his usual concert showcase for the next three years. Amusingly, on the road Ringo usually managed to forget that the song had all of two verses, and ended up repeating the first one over and over again.

DEVIL IN HER HEART
RICHARD DRAPKIN
RECORDED 18 JULY 1963

Aficionados of the American girl-group sound, The Beatles borrowed this tune from The Donays – probably the most obscure song they ever covered in the studio. It was George Harrison's choice, and he responded with an energetic if not always convincing lead vocal, backed by the superb chorus harmonies of Lennon and McCartney.

NOT A SECOND TIME
JOHN LENNON/PAUL McCARTNEY
RECORDED 11 SEPTEMBER 1963

'Not A Second Time' reinforced John Lennon's status as the most adventurous of The Beatles when it came to composing. The rhythm of this piano-based song seemed to be on the verge of imminent collapse, but whereas this was a flaw on 'Ask Me Why', it suited the emotional disruption of the lyric this time around. Usually, John sounded completely in control of every romantic situation, even when the lyrics asserted otherwise, but everything about 'Not A Second Time' announced that Lennon was simply a pawn in her game, predating the more blatant emotional masochism of 'Norwegian Wood' by two years.

MONEY (THAT'S WHAT I WANT)
BERRY GORDY/JANIE BRADFORD
RECORDED 18, 30 JULY, 30 SEPTEMBER 1963

The third and last of the Motown classics moulded into pure John Lennon songs, Barrett Strong's hit 'Money' took on a new life in this interpretation. The tentative delivery of the original was knocked off the pavement by Lennon's steamroller vocal, every bit as tonsil-shredding as 'Twist And Shout' had been. As on 'I Wanna Be Your Man', George Martin came into his own on keyboards: on the earlier track, he'd played Hammond organ, while this time he supplied the piano which was the root of the song.

But the piano wasn't the only difference between this performance, and the far less convincing version of the same tune at The Beatles' January 1962 audition. At Decca, Lennon had simply been singing Barrett Strong's song. At EMI nearly two years later, he was living it, howling the lyrics as a piece of psychotherapy. And as many critics have noticed, he widened the context of the song by adding a single, throwaway phrase to the final choruses: "I wanna be free", he cried, a prisoner to the passion that the rest of the song denied.

Trivial note: mono and stereo mixes of this song once again have slightly different Lennon vocals. And once again, the definitive version is included on the mono-only CD.

A Hard Day's Night

PARLOPHONE

CDP7 46437 2

The transition from pop stars to film actors was already a well-trodden route by 1964. The pop business hadn't yet cottoned on to the potential riches of international merchandising, but a hasty and cheap black-and-white movie was the next best thing. It also enabled The Beatles to be seen in towns and countries that they had no intention of visiting in person. It's probably not a coincidence that The Beatles staged only one further lengthy UK tour after the A Hard Day's Night film was released.

Although the film grossed millions of dollars in America, it was originally conceived as an entirely British phenomenon. The Beatles had been approached in the autumn of 1963, at which stage their fame had scarcely spread beyond their native land. Hence the low budget and black-and-white film: if United Artists had realised the movie would never be shown in America, they would almost certainly have ensured it was made in colour.

"We were a bit infuriated by the glibness of it and the shittiness of the dialogue," John Lennon complained in 1970. But Alun Owen's script was a work of remarkable realism by the previous standards of British pop films. The Beatles played caricatures of themselves, in caricatures of their everyday situations – on the road, in concert, and rehearsing for a TV show. Several scenes in the movie featured the group's earlier hits, but the contract called for the band to supply director Dick Lester with seven new songs; and EMI soon made the decision to release a soundtrack album, which would feature the film songs alongside another batch of new recordings.

Returning from their first visit to the States, The Beatles were faced with a ridiculously tight schedule. They had less than two weeks to write and record the songs for the film; then, during the subsequent shooting, they had to knock off the remaining numbers for the album. If ever there was an excuse for recording cover versions, this was it: instead, for the first and only time in The Beatles' career, John Lennon and Paul McCartney wrote the entire album between them. "Between them" was hardly correct, in fact, as Lennon contributed no fewer than ten of the thirteen tracks, dominating the LP more than any one Beatle was ever allowed to do thereafter.

Once again, The Beatles okayed the mono mix of the album, and then left George Martin to prepare a hasty stereo version; and once again, Martin utilised the mono tracks on EMI's CD release.

A HARD DAY'S NIGHT
JOHN LENNON/PAUL McCARTNEY
RECORDED 16 APRIL 1964

Ringo Starr, recalling some wordplay of John Lennon's, inadvertently christened The Beatles' first film, saving it from the fate of going into history as *Beatlemania*. Once the

title was fixed, The Beatles had to provide a song to match, and quickly: within a week, Lennon (with help from McCartney on the middle section) had prepared this sturdy piece of songwriting-to-order.

The unforgettable opening – George Harrison striking a G suspended 4th chord on his 12-string Rickenbacker – took a few takes to get right, but eventually made this record one of the few that can be recognised by its opening two seconds alone.

For the first time, Lennon and McCartney settled into the pattern they would follow for the rest of the group's lifetime, each man singing the section of the song he'd written. Fans had an early chance to distinguish between McCartney's in-born lyrical optimism, and Lennon's grudging cynicism. And there was another revolution in the air, as The Beatles discovered the joys of fading their singles out, rather than ending in a single climactic chord. After double-tracking and overdubbing, fade-outs became the next favourite toy in The Beatles' studio cupboard.

I SHOULD HAVE KNOWN BETTER

JOHN LENNON/PAUL McCARTNEY

RECORDED 26 FEBRUARY 1964

Even when he was functioning as an admitted hack writer, composing Beatles songs to a tight deadline, the John Lennon of 1964 succeeded effortlessly in concocting memorable melody lines. 'I Should Have Known Better' was built around the simplest of two-chord rhythms, with puffing harmonica to match, but it had an effervescence that touched everything The Beatles recorded in the heady spring of 1964.

IF I FELL

JOHN LENNON/PAUL McCARTNEY

RECORDED 27 FEBRUARY 1964

In 1964, no-one had yet noticed any split in songwriting styles between Lennon and McCartney, so this delicate and melodic ballad was greeted as just another Beatles song. Only in retrospect was it seen as early proof that there was more to John Lennon's armoury than rock'n'roll, acid imagery and cynical wit. In structural terms, this was by far the most complex song John had written to date, and its terrifyingly high harmony line briefly floored McCartney, whose voice cracked under the strain on the mix released on the stereo album. On the CD and the mono LP, however, Paul walked the tightrope without missing a note.

I'M HAPPY JUST TO DANCE WITH YOU

JOHN LENNON/PAUL McCARTNEY

RECORDED 1 MARCH 1964

John Lennon wrote this song, but thought so little of it that he passed it over for George Harrison to sing – The Beatles' lead guitarist having failed to meet with group approval for any of his latest efforts at songwriting. Lennon would no doubt have regarded the song's theme as too tame for his more rugged image – though he *had* just reached the top of the American charts by saying he wanted to hold his girl's hand – but Harrison's charmingly naïve vocal delivery caught the mood of the song perfectly. As usual, The Beatles patched up the thinnest of material with a superlatively commercial arrangement.

AND I LOVE HER
JOHN LENNON/PAUL McCARTNEY
RECORDED 27 FEBRUARY 1964

Even under pressure, The Beatles refused to settle for anything but the best when recording this McCartney love song for his girlfriend of the time, actress Jane Asher. For three days running, they attempted different arrangements, eventually nailing it in the same three-hour session in which they cut 'Tell Me Why'. Simple, evocative and gentler than any Lennon/McCartney song they'd recorded up to that point, 'And I Love Her' was treated to a predominantly acoustic arrangement.

Trivia note: several different edits of this song were released in different parts of the world, the variations coming in the number of times the closing guitar riff was repeated.

TELL ME WHY
JOHN LENNON/PAUL McCARTNEY
RECORDED 27 FEBRUARY 1964

Another delicious piece of hackwork, 'Tell Me Why' was almost Beatles by numbers – a beefy chorus, a wonderfully cool Lennon vocal, even a self-mocking falsetto section towards the end, and all wrapped up in a fraction over two minutes.

CAN'T BUY ME LOVE
JOHN LENNON/PAUL McCARTNEY
RECORDED 29 JANUARY 1964

The Beatles' first single of 1964 was taped almost as an afterthought, at the end of the group's one and only EMI studio session outside Britain. Their visit to Pathé Marconi Studios in Paris had been arranged so they could reluctantly concoct German-language versions of two of their biggest hits. With less than an hour remaining, the group cut this Paul McCartney song in just four takes – completely reworking the arrangement between their first, R&B-styled attempt and the more polished final version.

'Can't Buy Me Love' came closer than any of The Beatles' singles thus far, to matching the rock'n'roll music that they'd been playing since the mid-50s. Its lyrics neatly reversed the theme of 'Money' from their previous album, and the track gave George Harrison a splendid opportunity to show off his guitar skills. He added his solo as an overdub, having already proved on that tentative first take that unrehearsed improvisation wasn't exactly his forte.

ANY TIME AT ALL
JOHN LENNON/PAUL McCARTNEY
RECORDED 2 JUNE 1964

Tight for time, as they were at every session in 1964, The Beatles began recording this song before John Lennon had finished writing it. Thankfully, they eventually realised the fact, though not before they'd attempted seven takes. Lennon added a gentle middle section to this otherwise tough rocker during their afternoon tea-break, and the song was in the can well before bedtime.

I'LL CRY INSTEAD
JOHN LENNON/PAUL McCARTNEY
RECORDED 1 JUNE 1964

Though The Beatles' sound is commonly regarded as a mix of American rock'n'roll, pop and R&B, country music became a vital part of the equation from 1964. Under a constant barrage of encouragement from Ringo Starr, the rest of the group started listening to records by Buck Owens, George Jones and other Nashville stars, and the influence began to filter through to the songwriting – particularly Lennon's.

For such a simple song, 'I'll Cry Instead' proved tough to record. Eventually The Beatles gave up trying to perform it live, and divided it into two sections, which George Martin edited together as the final record. Its divided nature explains why it was so easy for the song to be artificially extended for the US album release.

'I'll Cry Instead' inadvertently spawned a genre of Beatles and solo songs: lyrics which had Lennon, usually the masterful romantic hero, sitting head in hands, indulging himself in an ocean of self-pity. For much of the last decade of his life, this pose of guilt and sorrow became something of a straitjacket around his songwriting.

THINGS WE SAID TODAY
JOHN LENNON/PAUL McCARTNEY
RECORDED 2 JUNE 1964

McCartney's contributions to 'A Hard Day's Night' may have been few in number, but they were impressively strong. Like John, Paul was experimenting with writing around minor chords, and quickly realised that they lent themselves to lyrics that were reflective rather than celebratory. John took the formula a stage further by writing almost all his songs for this album in the key of G.

WHEN I GET HOME
JOHN LENNON/PAUL McCARTNEY
RECORDED 2 JUNE 1964

Like much of his work on this album, 'When I Get Home' doesn't bear too much critical examination – except that from a hastily assembled song, The Beatles were able to make a state-of-the-art pop record by 1964 standards. The track began as if in mid-performance, with a catchy vocal hook, and then romped along merrily enough for another two minutes, without ever suggesting that Lennon meant a word he was singing.

YOU CAN'T DO THAT
JOHN LENNON/PAUL McCARTNEY
RECORDED 25 FEBRUARY, 22 MAY 1964

Of all the songs on this album, John Lennon was proudest of this. Not at all coincidentally, it was the roughest, least polished number he'd recorded up to that date. It was blatantly inspired by the R&B songs coming out of Memphis, and (as rock critic Lester Bangs wrote years later), "built on one of the bitterest and most iron-indestructible riffs ever conceived". Lennon handled the lead guitar himself, hammering out a wiry solo which grew into a furious flurry of chords, totally unlike anything that George Harrison had performed on the rest of the album.

I'LL BE BACK
JOHN LENNON/PAUL McCARTNEY
RECORDED 1 JUNE 1964

At the end of a record that was a brilliant collection of sometimes less than brilliant songs, John Lennon's 'I'll Be Back' harked back to the strange construction of some of his earlier efforts. Like 'Ask Me Why' and 'All I've Got To Do', it was pure Lennon, owing nothing to what was happening in the pop world around him. For the moment, he hadn't hit on the knack of combining these unsettling melodies with words that carried any emotional weight, so 'I'll Be Back' ended up another superb song about a fictional romance. But the moment of liberation wasn't far away.

PARLOPHONE
MADE AND IN
THE PARLOPHONE CO. LTD.
AUSTRALIA (PROPRIETARY)

EMI
THE GREATEST RECORDING
ORGANIZATION IN THE WORLD

BEATLES
FOR
SALE

Beatles For Sale

PARLOPHONE

CDP7 46438 2

It's been noted before that the tired, glazed expressions of the four Beatles on the cover of their fourth album was a simple response to circumstances. Unlike the pampered stars of the 90s, they had no chance between 1963 and 1965 to bask in their wealth and fame. They toured almost non-stop through 1963, breaking only for an occasional week's rest – during which they were expected to write and record, tape radio shows for the BBC, and meet the press. 1964 began the same way: two weeks in a Christmas Show at the Astoria, Finsbury Park, then three weeks in France, a fortnight in the States, a week to start work on the soundtrack to A Hard Day's Night, and then an intensive two months of filming. Aside from a holiday in May, their year followed this hectic course right to the end, encompassing a second visit to America, a tour of Australia and New Zealand, a quick jaunt across Europe, summer seaside dates in Engand, and finally a five-week series of UK concerts in October and November.

Into that schedule had to be squeezed the recording of the aptly titled 'Beatles For Sale'. It was thrown together on off-days between concerts over a period of almost three months, so it wasn't altogether surprising when the record seemed to take a step back from the stylistic unity of their earlier LPs. The return to a blend of original material and covers hinted at the strain the group were under; the generally perfunctory nature of their cov-ers rammed the message home. But the eight Lennon/McCartney songs on the album dis-played a growing maturity, and betrayed a new set of influences which would very soon whisk The Beatles beyond the reach of their beat group contemporaries.

One of the prime inspirations for the 'Beatles For Sale' songs was country music – first noted on 'I'll Cry Instead' on the third album, and a constant point of reference through their work in 1965. The group had grown up on rockabilly, itself deeply rooted in country, but it took Ringo's continual championing of Nashville's contemporary stars to inspire songs like 'I Don't Want To Spoil The Party' and 'Baby's In Black'.

More lasting was the creative impact of Bob Dylan, to whom The Beatles had been listening since the end of 1963. At first, Lennon, McCartney and Harrison picked up on the style and sound of Dylan's records. Once the American singer had introduced them to the pleasures of dope, however, they began to respond to the artistic freedom that his songwriting made possible. Without Dylan, or drugs, the path from 'Beatles For Sale' to 'Revolver' might have been too tangled for The Beatles to follow.

Apparently, before that he thought my songs tended to sort of wander off." Music publisher Dick James soon found his own tastes outstripped by the adventurous spirit of The Beatles; by 1966, no-one was looking to their songs for "a complete story". But James was right on one score: even though the song was plainly a piece of romantic fiction, it had a watertight structure and a powerful melody, and The Beatles' skills as vocal arrangers were on open display. On tracks like this, 'Beatles For Sale' sounds like the pinnacle of British beat music, polished to an icy sheen in preparation for being shattered by The Beatles and the Stones, among others, over the next 12 months.

'No Reply' would go on to become the favoured track for owners of answerphones to record on their machines 20 years later.

NO REPLY
JOHN LENNON/PAUL McCARTNEY
RECORDED 30 SEPTEMBER 1964

"I remember Dick James coming to me after we did this one," John Lennon recalled shortly before his death, "and saying, 'You're getting much better now – this is a complete story'.

I'M A LOSER
JOHN LENNON/PAUL McCARTNEY
RECORDED 14 AUGUST 1964

Looking back at this song, Lennon recognised it as a milestone. "Instead of projecting myself into a situation," he explained, "I would try to

THE BEATLES : BEATLES FOR SALE

express what I felt about myself. I think it was Dylan who helped me realise that." And the Dylan influence was obvious in other ways, too, from the acoustic guitars powering the song to the use of the harmonica as a statement of passion.

Like 'I'll Cry Instead', 'I'm A Loser' soon drifted into naked self-pity – and anyway, the raw emotions of the song were dressed up in a strong pop format. But for a while, at least, Lennon was delighted at his discovery that he could channel his innermost thoughts into music, as well as the free-form linguistic pleasures of his books. As for the song's message, Lennon summed up his ambivalence perfectly in 1970: "Part of me thinks I'm a loser and part of me thinks I'm God Almighty".

BABY'S IN BLACK
JOHN LENNON/PAUL McCARTNEY
RECORDED 11 AUGUST 1964

A heavy waltz with a vague country influence, 'Baby's In Black' was one of the last genuine Lennon/McCartney collaborations – composed during a head-to-head session over acoustic guitars, the way they'd been doing

since the late 50s. Its rather maudlin lyric suggests that it might originally have been a Lennon idea, but the performance is pure Beatles – and pure 1964. Numbers like this, which invested a little romantic difficulty with the importance of a world crisis, gradually faded from The Beatles' repertoire over the next twelve months.

ROCK AND ROLL MUSIC
CHUCK BERRY
RECORDED 18 OCTOBER 1964

Not for the first time, The Beatles took a classic American record and cut it to shreds. Chuck Berry's original Chess recording – which set up rock'n'roll as an antidote to boredom with every other musical style – only hinted at the raw power of the genre. With Lennon, McCartney and producer George Martin trebling up the keyboard part, The Beatles made every hint of that promise into reality. Berry wrote and performed brilliant rock songs, but it took Lennon to sing this one the way it was meant to be heard.

I'LL FOLLOW THE SUN
JOHN LENNON/PAUL McCARTNEY
RECORDED 18 OCTOBER 1964

As early as 1960, the pre-Beatles Liverpool band, The Quarry Men, were experimenting with a tentative arrangement of this McCartney song, making it just about the earliest Lennon/McCartney composition which they ever recorded. Simple but effortlessly melodic, it proves that Paul was born with the gift of writing memorable tunes, while John Lennon's ability as a tunesmith evolved only with practice.

MR. MOONLIGHT
ROY LEE JOHNSON
RECORDED 18 OCTOBER 1964

On Friday August 14, 1964, The Beatles recorded one of the strongest rock'n'roll performances of their career. Sadly, this wasn't it. But it could have been: the group eventually decided to jettison their electrifying interpretation of Little Willie John's R&B standard, 'Leave My Kitten Alone' (which remains officially unreleased) in favour of this bizarre, mediocre version of another song

from black America, Dr. Feelgood & The Interns' 'Mr. Moonlight'.

John Lennon had taken to the song immediately he heard it, and it was swiftly incorporated into their Cavern repertoire. But the recorded version, which required two separate sessions to 'perfect', had none of the spontaneity or humour of their live performances. It shambled along rather apologetically, and the half-hearted vocal support from McCartney and Harrison left Lennon's impassioned lead sounding faintly ridiculous. Asked to pick the weakest track The Beatles ever recorded, a fair percentage of fans would opt for 'Mr. Moonlight'.

KANSAS CITY/HEY, HEY, HEY, HEY
JERRY LEIBER/MIKE STOLLER
RICHARD PENNIMAN
RECORDED 18 OCTOBER 1964

Like Little Richard before them, The Beatles covered Leiber and Stoller's early 50s R&B song and added a frenetic call-and-response routine to the end. Richard had already reworked the original arrangement to his own specifications, and Paul McCartney followed that revamp to the letter. For this recording, The Beatles simply blasted the song the way they did on stage. This late 1964 rendition may be tighter than the performance from December 1962 captured on the '1962 Live Recordings' CD, but the approach is almost identical.

EIGHT DAYS A WEEK
JOHN LENNON/PAUL McCARTNEY
RECORDED 6, 18 OCTOBER 1964

A few months earlier, The Beatles had been delighted by the discovery that they could fade their recordings out. Now they went a stage further, and made pop history by fading this song *in*. Ironically, the track had a conventional ending – though that was edited onto the tape after the basic recording was finished.

Like 'Baby's In Black', 'Eight Days A Week' was a Lennon/McCartney collaboration, though again with Lennon's influence to the fore. It would have made a perfect hit single, and may even have been written with that idea in mind, as its title obviously has some link with the working name of their second movie,

scripts for which had already been submitted by October 1964: *Eight Arms To Hold You*.

WORDS OF LOVE
BUDDY HOLLY
RECORDED 18 OCTOBER 1964

Two standards from The Beatles' pre-fame live repertoire went through a change of ownership during these sessions. Back at the Cavern in 1961 and 1962, it had been Lennon and Harrison who shared the close harmony vocals on this Buddy Holly song – the only number by one of their favourite writers that they ever recorded. On the record, though, which kept strictly to Holly's arrangement, McCartney elbowed Harrison out of the limelight. Nevertheless, George's contribution – the lovely chiming guitar licks throughout – is pretty impressive.

HONEY DON'T
CARL PERKINS
RECORDED 26 OCTOBER 1964

The second change came with this Carl Perkins rockabilly favourite – traditionally sung by John Lennon on stage, but passed over amiably to Ringo Starr as his token vocal cameo on the album. The switch gave Ringo the chance to utter one of his trademark invitations to George as Harrison launched into the guitar solo.

EVERY LITTLE THING
JOHN LENNON/PAUL McCARTNEY
RECORDED 30 SEPTEMBER 1964

Though it's one of the least well-known songs they ever recorded, John Lennon's 'Every Little Thing' was as impressive as anything on 'Beatles For Sale', with all the trademarks of their 1964 work – a laconic, yet affectionate Lennon vocal, some Harrison guitar that looked forward to the as-yet-unrecorded sound of The Byrds, and a stunningly melodic chorus that stuck instantly in the brain. Ripe for rediscovery by someone like Tom Petty (and covered in 1969 by Yes, of all people), it justifies the claim that almost every Lennon/McCartney song on The Beatles' early albums would have made a convincing hit single.

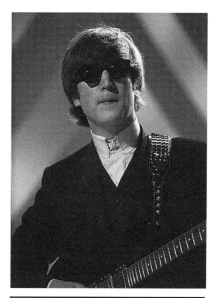

I DON'T WANT TO SPOIL THE PARTY
JOHN LENNON/PAUL McCARTNEY
RECORDED 29 SEPTEMBER 1964

Influenced partly by rockabilly, partly by mainstream country, and partly by the general air of melancholy that seeped into several of his songs in 1964, John Lennon wrote this vaguely self-pitying account of romantic disappointment. Proof of The Beatles' increasing sophistication as arrangers came with the middle eight, on which Paul's harmony moved subtly away from the simple line he might have sung a year earlier.

WHAT YOU'RE DOING
JOHN LENNON/PAUL McCARTNEY
RECORDED 26 OCTOBER 1964

With 'I'll Follow The Sun' having been written in the late 50s, 'What You're Doing' proved to be Paul McCartney's only new solo contribution to the 'Beatles For Sale' album. After outstripping Lennon as a songwriter in the group's early years, Paul was now going through a fallow period, just when John was at his most prolific. A couple of years later, the situation would be dramatically reversed.

The song itself was built around a simple guitar riff, but as often proves to be the case, simplicity proved difficult to perfect. The Beatles devoted two sessions to taping the song before junking the results and then recutting it on the last possible day of recording.

EVERYBODY'S TRYING TO BE MY BABY
CARL PERKINS
RECORDED 18 OCTOBER 1964

Cut in a single, echo-swamped take, this second Carl Perkins cover allowed George Harrison the chance to pay his respects to one of his all-time musical heroes. The combination of the disorientating echo and Harrison's scouse drawl made Perkins' overtly Tennessean lyrics almost impossible to decipher: without access to a lyric sheet, in fact, Harrison may simply have been reproducing the sound of what the American rocker was singing, rather than exactly the same words. Either way, it made for a strange ending to a disjointed album.

THE BEATLES stereo

HELP!

Help!

PARLOPHONE

CDP7 46439 2

A vastly increased budget, colour stock, exotic overseas locations, and a lavish publicity campaign – The Beatles' second feature film had everything except the one quality which had made its predecessor so successful, realism. John Lennon later dismissed Help! as "bullshit", which was unjustly harsh. But though its script crackled with jokes and The Beatles wisecracked their way through the full 100 minutes, complete with striking musical interludes, Help! didn't have the magic of A Hard Day's Night. That's not to say it wasn't a successful movie by its own lights. It grossed an impressive figure, in Britain and around the world, and it stands up today as a glossy, semi-satirical period piece, perfectly in keeping with the wacky Beatles image that the world initially mistook for the real thing.

By 1965, though, The Beatles were losing interest in refuelling their image. Through the use of soft drugs, they were beginning to glimpse an artistic purpose beyond Beatlemania and the production-line of hit records. John Lennon, in particular, managed in 1965 to find his own lyrical voice, and started to use The Beatles as a vehicle to express his increasingly confused feelings about his role in the group, and his personal relationships.

In one important respect, the preparations for Help! were identical to those for the previous year's movie. The decision was made in advance to divide the 'soundtrack' album between one side of songs that would appear in the film, and another of non-movie tunes. And as before, the film songs had to be completed before the shooting began. The Beatles' flight for the Bahamas left on February 22: just seven days earlier, the group arrived for their first movie session at Abbey Road. By the time their plane set off for their film location, they had recorded no fewer than 11 songs — although two of these, 'If You've Got Trouble' and 'That Means A Lot', were destined to remain unreleased.

At that stage, the film was still untitled, and it wasn't until The Beatles had returned to Britain at the end of March that they were informed that it would be called *Help!*. A title song was commissioned and delivered almost overnight, while the soundtrack album was eventually completed during breaks in the filming, just six weeks before its release date.

HELP!
JOHN LENNON/PAUL McCARTNEY
RECORDED 13 APRIL 1965

"The only true songs I ever wrote were 'Help!' and 'Strawberry Fields'," John Lennon claimed in December 1970. "They were the ones I really wrote from experience and not projecting myself into a situation and writing a nice story about it, which I always found phoney. The lyric is as good now as it was then. It makes me feel secure to know that I was that sensible, aware of myself back then. But I don't like the recording that much, we did

it too fast, to try to be commercial." In the same week he gave that interview, Lennon actually attempted to re-record the song, slowing it to funereal pace as a piano ballad. His efforts merely exposed what a smooth and powerful piece of work The Beatles' rendition was – to the point that the surface sheen and production expertise successfully disguised any hint of authentic anguish in Lennon's vocal. The record turned out nothing more or less than a perfect Beatles single, and an ideal theme tune for their movie.

Trivia note: the single and LP versions of this song feature slightly different Lennon vocals.

THE NIGHT BEFORE
JOHN LENNON/PAUL McCARTNEY
RECORDED 17 FEBRUARY 1965

Studio finesse was second nature to The Beatles by February 1965 – and so too was commercial songwriting. John Lennon's first flirtation with electric piano (which was a constant feature on this album) was the only novel moment on this fluent and ultra-appealing McCartney pop song.

YOU'VE GOT TO HIDE YOUR LOVE AWAY

JOHN LENNON/PAUL McCARTNEY

RECORDED 18 FEBRUARY 1965

After the tentative Dylan-isms of 'I'm A Loser', John Lennon made his debt to the American singer-songwriter entirely clear on this song. Too self-pitying for Dylan himself, it was nonetheless a piece of personal expression for its composer, who still automatically equated writing from the heart with songs about romantic disappointment.

For two musical reasons, this track stood out from earlier Beatles recordings. First of all, it was an entirely acoustic performance from an electric rock'n'roll band. Secondly, it featured a guest musician from outside The Beatles' circle. George Martin had been adding keyboards to the group's records from the start, but this song featured a flute solo by arranger John Scott, though his contribution wasn't noted on the sleeve.

I NEED YOU

GEORGE HARRISON

RECORDED 15, 16 FEBRUARY 1965

For only the second time, The Beatles recorded a George Harrison composition – earlier efforts like 'You'll Know What To Do' having been rejected by Lennon/McCartney. An otherwise unexceptional song was punctuated by brief, slightly hesitant bursts of guitar noise, controlled by a foot pedal soon to become famous as the wah-wah.

ANOTHER GIRL

JOHN LENNON/PAUL McCARTNEY

RECORDED 15, 16 FEBRUARY 1965

Though the songs themselves broke few boundaries, the recording sessions for the 'Help!' album found The Beatles gradually exploring new techniques and instrumental combinations. On his own 'Another Girl', for instance, Paul played the twisting lead guitar line – as he did on 'Ticket To Ride', recorded at the same session. George Harrison's misgivings about his diminished role on these tracks were presumably dampened by the fact that the third song taped that day was one of his own

YOU'RE GONNA LOSE THAT GIRL

JOHN LENNON/PAUL McCARTNEY

RECORDED 19 FEBRUARY 1965

A beautifully compact piece of songwriting, 'You're Gonna Lose That Girl' illustrated that Lennon was every bit McCartney's match when it came to producing quality pop tunes to order. Tempted though he must have been, Paul let George play lead guitar this time around, contenting himself with adding piano to the basic track.

TICKET TO RIDE

JOHN LENNON/PAUL McCARTNEY

RECORDED 15 FEBRUARY 1965

John Lennon once described this song, The Beatles' first single of 1965, as the precursor to heavy metal. "It was pretty fucking heavy for then," he boasted, "if you go and look at what other people were making. It doesn't sound too bad." Indeed not: from Lennon's brilliantly deadpan vocal to Ringo's cross-beat drumming and McCartney's lead guitar flourishes, 'Ticket To Ride' was musically the strongest record The Beatles had made up to that point.

ACT NATURALLY

JOHNNY RUSSELL/VONIE HARRISON

RECORDED 17 JUNE 1965

Ringo's usual vocal appearance on this album was originally supposed to be 'If You've Got Trouble', a dire Lennon/McCartney composition which The Beatles attempted twice before recognising its canine qualities. By way of compensation for being saddled with such a loser, Ringo was allowed to record an American country hit, co-written by comedian Johnny Russell, and recently débuted by one of the giants of the Bakersfield sound, Buck Owens. With its "they're gonna put me in the movies" lyric, the song fitted the bill perfectly. More than two decades later, Ringo and Buck combined forces to re-record the number.

IT'S ONLY LOVE

JOHN LENNON/PAUL McCARTNEY

RECORDED 15 JUNE 1965

Asked to select his least favourite Beatles songs, John Lennon went unerringly for 'Run For Your Life' and this mawkish number – which was still considered strong enough to qualify for heartfelt cover versions by vocalists

as diverse as Bryan Ferry and Gary 'US' Bonds. Listen out again for George Harrison on wah-wah guitar, this song being one of the least likely candidates for such an effect in the entire Beatles catalogue.

YOU LIKE ME TOO MUCH
GEORGE HARRISON
RECORDED 17 FEBRUARY 1965

American rock critic Lester Bangs noted that this George Harrison composition was "probably the first song in rock history whose lyrics admitted that neither party loved the other but neither had the guts to call it quits". Harrison's unsentimental attitude to love resurfaced on the next album with 'If I Needed Someone'. At the time, though, more attention was paid to George's increasing confidence as a vocalist, and to the two-men-at-one-piano trick of Paul and George Martin.

TELL ME WHAT YOU SEE
JOHN LENNON/PAUL McCARTNEY
RECORDED 18 FEBRUARY 1965

More electric piano, and another McCartney pop tune, slightly more laboured than its contemporaries on this record. The 'Help!' album was the last occasion on which The Beatles felt able to indulge themselves in a set of entirely fictional teen-romance songwriting. By the time they reconvened for the 'Rubber Soul' sessions at the end of 1965, the con-

cept of lyric-writing as a form of intimate confession had taken hold.

I'VE JUST SEEN A FACE
JOHN LENNON/PAUL McCARTNEY
RECORDED 14 JUNE 1965

A folk song taken at bluegrass tempo, 'I've Just Seen A Face' was a McCartney gem, given an entirely satisfactory acoustic arrangement. The fact that it was taped during the same three-hour session as Paul's screaming rocker, 'I'm Down', makes its discreet assurance even more remarkable.

Paul resurrected this song during the Wings' tours of the mid-Seventies.

YESTERDAY
JOHN LENNON/PAUL McCARTNEY
RECORDED 14 JUNE 1965

"I really reckon 'Yesterday' is probably my best song," said Paul McCartney in 1980. "I like it not only because it was a big success, but because it was one of the most instinctive songs I've ever written. I was so proud of it. I felt it was an original tune – the most complete thing I've ever written. It's very catchy without being sickly."

Despite his initial misgivings about the song's sentimentality, John Lennon eventually agreed, picking 'Yesterday' as one of Paul's strongest compositions. Its origins have passed into the realms of legend: McCartney awoke one morning with the melody in his head, set some nonsense words to the tune to make sure he remembered it (working title: 'Scrambled Egg') and then played it to all and sundry, convinced that a song which had come so easily must have been stolen from something else. No one could identify the source, and Paul was eventually convinced that 'Yesterday' had sprung fully-formed from his own imagination.

In 1965, the song evoked some controversy, when it was revealed to the press that Paul had recorded it without any help from the rest of the group, the only instrumental support coming from his own acoustic guitar and a string quartet arranged by George Martin. American magazines listed the song as a McCartney solo release, and when it topped the US singles charts there was

speculation that Paul would soon opt for a career outside the group. So he did, but not for another five years.

DIZZY MISS LIZZY
LARRY WILLIAMS
RECORDED 10 MAY 1965

Larry Williams emerged from the same Specialty Records stable as Little Richard, and his best records shared Richard's frenetic marriage of rock'n'roll and R&B. McCartney handled the Little Richard covers in The Beatles, while the Larry Williams songs became Lennon's responsibility. The group had been performing 'Dizzy Miss Lizzy' on stage since their first trip to Hamburg in 1960, though Harrison's slightly erratic guitar fills showed that they hadn't played it for a while before this session. But Lennon cruised through the vocal like the natural rock'n'roller he was.

He illustrated his love for the song by reviving it at his first major post-Beatles concert appearance in Toronto four years later. Meanwhile, 'Dizzy Miss Lizzy' became the last cover version that The Beatles ever released.

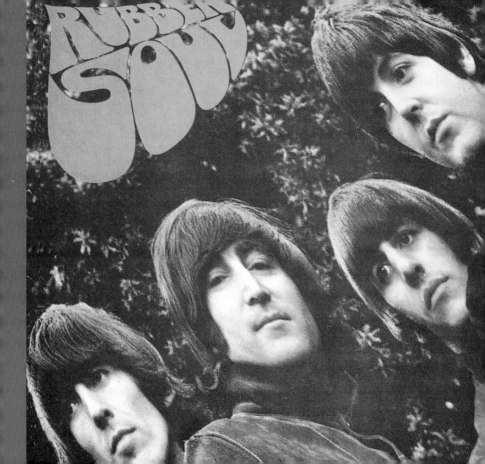

Rubber Soul

PARLOPHONE
CDP7 46440 2

" **I** think 'Rubber Soul' was the first of The Beatles' albums which presented a new Beatles to the world," reckons George Martin, who was close enough to the proceedings to know. "Up till then, we had been making albums rather like a collection of singles. Now we were really beginning to think about albums as a bit of art on their own. And 'Rubber Soul' was the first to emerge that way." John Lennon concurred: "We were just getting better, technically and musically, that's all. We finally took over the studio. On 'Rubber Soul', we were sort of more precise about making the album, and we took over the cover and everything. It was Paul's album title, just a pun. There is no great mysterious meaning behind all this, it was just four boys, working out what to call a new album." There's no real disagreement, among fans, musicians and critics alike. 'Sgt. Pepper' may have been The Beatles' production extravaganza, and 'Revolver' their first post-acid celebration, but 'Rubber Soul' was the record on which they revealed clear signs of fresh thinking – not just in musical or lyrical terms, but also philosophically. If 'Beatles For Sale' marked the pinnacle of British beat, and 'Help!' a consolidation of the past, 'Rubber Soul' was a step into the future.

It's important to remember that The Beatles weren't pioneers in their quest for new artistic experiences. Bob Dylan had already recorded and released 'Bringing It All Back Home' and 'Highway 61 Revisited' by the time the group began work on 'Rubber Soul'. But The Beatles were the first to introduce Dylan's free-form wordplay into the tight constraints of the three-minute pop song. Weeks before The Byrds discovered the joys of being 'Eight Miles High', the Liverpudlians announced that "the word is love".

Equally important to remember is that, unlike 'Pepper' or 'The White Album',

'Rubber Soul' wasn't a carefully considered studio creation. As they had been the previous autumn, The Beatles were trapped on a deadline-powered treadmill. When they arrived at Abbey Road studios on October 12, they knew that their next single, and album, had to be ready for release at the start of December. In the event, they cut it right to the bone: the final songs weren't written or recorded until mid-November. Just 18 days after the album was mixed, copies were on sale in the shops.

Despite the determinedly trend-setting approach of the album, one thing hadn't changed: The Beatles still intended 'Rubber Soul' to be heard in mono, rather than stereo. In order to make both this record and 'Help!' acceptable for modern digital audiences, George Martin remixed them both into 'proper' stereo for the CD releases.

wrote The Beatles' most raucous songs of 1965 – 'I'm Down' (the flipside of the 'Help!' single) and then this sly piece of sexual innuendo. What's most noticeable about the song at this distance, though, is the sparseness of the production. At a time when their nearest rivals, The Rolling Stones, were experimenting with dense, murky soundscapes, The Beatles cut this album with the maximum of separation between individual instruments, creating a feeling of space rather than tension.

DRIVE MY CAR
JOHN LENNON/PAUL McCARTNEY
RECORDED 13 OCTOBER 1965

For all John Lennon's reputation as a rock'n'roller, it was Paul McCartney who

NORWEGIAN WOOD (THIS BIRD HAS FLOWN)
JOHN LENNON/PAUL McCARTNEY
RECORDED 21 OCTOBER 1965

At the time it was released, Paul McCartney described this Lennon composition as "a comedy song". In the same debunking spirit, George Harrison admitted that the arrangement was "an accident as far as the sitar part was concerned". And not until 1970 did John Lennon explain: "I was trying to write about an affair without letting my wife know I was writing about an affair."

The sitar wasn't an accident, as George had played the instrument on the first still unreleased version of the song on October 12. And the lyrics certainly weren't comedy, though they had their moments of humour. In oblique, memorable imagery, Lennon conjured up a romantic encounter that rapidly moved beyond his control – a theme that would soon become an obsession in his work.

YOU WON'T SEE ME
JOHN LENNON/PAUL McCARTNEY
RECORDED 11 NOVEMBER 1965

From reality to fantasy, in one fell swoop: no-one would claim McCartney's 'You Won't See Me' as a piece of self-revelation. But it was a supreme piece of commercial songwriting, recorded during the last, frantic day of sessions to complete the album. Note the superb falsetto harmonies, and McCartney's confident piano playing.

NOWHERE MAN
JOHN LENNON/PAUL McCARTNEY
RECORDED 21, 22 OCTOBER 1965

Sitting bored in his Surrey home suffering writer's block, John Lennon suddenly envisaged himself as the "nowhere man, thinking all his nowhere plans for nobody". As the composer, Lennon wrote himself a message of hope: "nowhere man, the world is at your command". The Beatles translated the song into gorgeous Byrdsian 1965 pop, showing off another set of delicious vocal harmonies.

THINK FOR YOURSELF
GEORGE HARRISON
RECORDED 8 NOVEMBER 1965

George Harrison's spiritual investigations would soon initiate an entire genre of songwriting. 'Think For Yourself' was the first sign that he had a voice of his own, every bit as cynical as Lennon's about the trappings of everyday life, but holding out the study of the mind and the universe as a panacea. "Try thinking more, if just for your own sake," he sang, in a line which summed up his philosophy for the next few years.

THE WORD
JOHN LENNON/PAUL McCARTNEY
RECORDED 10 NOVEMBER 1965

Meanwhile, John and Paul considered that "the word is love" – their first tentative step into the shimmering waters of drug-enhanced freedom and meditation. At the time, McCartney was more impressed by the song's simple musical form: "To write a good song with just one note in it – like 'Long Tall Sally' – is really very hard. It's the kind of thing we've wanted to do for some time. We get near it in 'The Word'."

MICHELLE
JOHN LENNON/PAUL McCARTNEY
RECORDED 3 NOVEMBER 1965

Songs become standards when they sound as if they've been around forever the first time you hear them. 1965 saw Paul McCartney unveiling the two songs that have been more covered than anything else he has ever written – first 'Yesterday' and then this romantic Gallic ballad, complete with in-built French translation. Every bit as much a hook as the chorus was the descending bass-line, as Paul explained to Mark Lewisohn: "I'll never forget

putting the bass line in because it was a kind of Bizet thing. It really turned the song around."

WHAT GOES ON
JOHN LENNON/PAUL McCARTNEY
RICHARD STARKEY
RECORDED 4 NOVEMBER 1965

"That was a very early song of mine," John Lennon explained, "but Ringo and Paul wrote a new middle eight together when we recorded it." That gave Ringo his first ever composing credit, the group having turned down his solitary composition up to that point, 'Don't Pass Me By'. On 'Rubber Soul', 'What Goes On' performed exactly the same function as 'Act Naturally' had on 'Help!' – opening the second side of the LP with a lightweight, country song in preparation for the meatier fare to follow.

GIRL
JOHN LENNON/PAUL McCARTNEY
RECORDED 11 NOVEMBER 1965

Written overnight for the last session of the album, 'Girl' was the song that illustrated just how far John Lennon had travelled since 'I Feel Fine' a year earlier. "'Girl' is real," he explained in 1970." It was about that girl, who happened to be Yoko in the end, the one that a lot of us were looking for. And I was trying to say something about Christianity, which I was opposed to at the time." With its biting attack on Catholic values, and its thinly veiled mixture of lust and disgust, 'Girl' was Lennon's most personal statement of disillusionment to date.

I'M LOOKING THROUGH YOU
JOHN LENNON/PAUL McCARTNEY
RECORDED 10, 11 NOVEMBER 1965

For almost the first time, Paul McCartney used this song as a vehicle for a personal message, rather than an attempt to write a hit single. He'd fallen out with his girlfriend of the time, Jane Asher, and 'I'm Looking Through You' was his response – half apology, half accusation. The Beatles first recorded the song without its melodic middle section, substituting a harsh guitar solo. Ever the tunesmith, Paul had written the missing lines by the time they finally recorded the released version.

IN MY LIFE
JOHN LENNON/PAUL McCARTNEY
RECORDED 18, 22 OCTOBER 1965

"In the early days, George Martin would translate for us," Lennon remembered in 1970. "In 'In My Life', there's an Elizabethan piano solo. He would do things like that." In musical terms, that was the most striking thing about 'In My Life'. But it acquired a new resonance in the wake of Lennon's death in 1980, when it took on the role of a personal epitaph, a warm-hearted salutation to friends and lovers down the years. That's the way it was intended in 1965, as well, with John feeling sufficiently removed from his upbringing to be able to feel nostalgic about the world he'd left behind.

WAIT
JOHN LENNON/PAUL McCARTNEY
RECORDED 17 JUNE, 11 NOVEMBER 1965

Desperate needs require desperate remedies, and for the second time ('Hold Me Tight' being the first) The Beatles plugged a gap on a new album by returning to a reject from a previous session. At least 'Hold Me Tight' had been re-recorded, though: for 'Wait', the group called up the tape of a song which they'd attempted during the sessions for 'Help!', and decided wasn't up to scratch. With more vocal harmonies, percussion and vocals, they salvaged it, though the song's naïve enthusiasm still sounds out-of-place amid the more worldly lyrics of other 'Rubber Soul' songs.

IF I NEEDED SOMEONE
GEORGE HARRISON
RECORDED 16, 18 OCTOBER 1965

By far the best song George Harrison had written up to that point, 'If I Needed Someone' left its mark for several reasons. It boasted stunning three-part harmonies, the tightest they'd yet achieved on record; it had a jingle-jangle guitar sound obviously borrowed from The Byrds, in exactly the same way as The Byrds had developed their sound from listening to The Beatles; and it featured lyrics that were not so much anti-romantic as totally realistic. 'If I Needed Someone' may be the first pop song written from the jaded, though not quite exhausted, viewpoint of a man who had women lined up outside his hotel door in every city of the world.

RUN FOR YOUR LIFE
JOHN LENNON/PAUL McCARTNEY
RECORDED 12 OCTOBER 1965

The first song to be recorded for 'Rubber Soul' appeared last on the album – and on its composer's list of preferences. "I always hated that one," John Lennon admitted in later years. "It was one I knocked off just to write a song, and it was phoney." It was also a mildly nasty rocker with a central threat stolen from an Elvis Presley classic. The line, "I'd rather see you dead little girl than to be with another man", first surfaced on Elvis's revolutionary revamp of the blues standard 'Baby, Let's Play House' back in 1955. Lennon never sought to disguise the theft; but in 1965, most reviewers and fans hadn't been schooled in Elvis's Sun sessions, which were then available only scattered across long-deleted albums, and the lyrical debt went unnoticed.

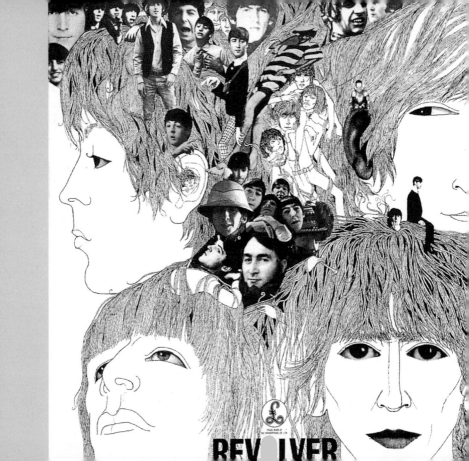

REVOLVER

Revolver

PARLOPHONE

CDP7 46441 2

The Beatles were supposed to begin 1966 by making their third feature film in as many years. But no-one could agree on a script, or even a theme, and instead The Beatles enjoyed an unprecedented three-month break at the start of the year. They were already convinced that their enervating routine of tour-film-record-tour had to be broken, and had completed their British tour at the end of 1965, assuming it would be their last. They were already contracted to undertake one final jaunt around the world in June, but mentally they were beginning to metamorphose into post-touring states of mind. With the exception of their last British concert at the NME Pollwinners' Show on May 1, The Beatles had more than two months on their schedule to record their next LP. They began on April 6th with the most revolutionary track on the album, Lennon's 'Tomorrow Never Knows', and ended just over eight weeks later with one of the two most brilliant pop albums ever recorded up to that point. Its rival was The Beach Boys' 'Pet Sounds', a masterpiece of melody, harmony and orchestral arrangement that undoubtedly affected the final sound of The Beatles' LP.

What time and mental space in the studio gave The Beatles was the chance to experiment (although most of the 'Revolver' songs went through remarkably little change of approach once the sessions began), and the freedom to choose exactly the right sound for each track. 'Revolver' was where The Beatles became a consummate studio band – ironically enough, in the same year that they proved completely unable (or maybe unwilling is closer to the point) to perform their more complex material on stage. Listen to 'Revolver', and then to the tuneless performances they gave on tour a few weeks later, and it's hard to imagine that they are the same band.

The Beatles' state of mind during that final tour is aptly summed up by this quote from Paul McCartney: "I was in Germany on tour just before 'Revolver' came out. I started listening to the album and I got really down because I thought the whole thing was out of tune. Everyone had to reassure me that it was OK." And so it was.

TAXMAN
GEORGE HARRISON
RECORDED 21, 22 APRIL, 16 MAY 1966

"'Taxman' was when I first realised that even though we had started earning money, we were actually giving most of it away in taxes." So said George Harrison, cementing forever the public perception of him as the Beatle most obsessed with money (an interesting sideline to his other clichéd role as the mystic Beatle). Groomed for years by manager Brian Epstein to stay out of political controversy, The Beatles began in 1966 to comment on issues like the war in Vietnam. 'Taxman' was a more universal protest – George fingered both the Conservative and Labour leaders in his lyrics – but the song had a political message,

nonetheless. It also had a remarkably powerful lead guitar riff, played (ironically enough) not by George but by Paul.

ELEANOR RIGBY
JOHN LENNON/PAUL McCARTNEY
RECORDED 28, 29 APRIL, 6 JUNE 1966

"I wrote a good half of the lyrics or more," claimed John Lennon in later years of this archetypal Paul McCartney song. True or not, it was a sign that Lennon realised the strength of what Paul had written. It was a short story with a moral, all packaged within little more than two minutes. Aside from the backing vocals, McCartney was the only Beatle featured on the track, accompanied by a string section scored by George Martin – one of his most obvious and effective contributions to a Beatles record. The song later inspired the most memorable segment of the *Yellow Submarine* movie, as the craft drifts above the lonely, dingy streets of Liverpool.

I'M ONLY SLEEPING

JOHN LENNON/PAUL McCARTNEY

RECORDED 27, 29 APRIL, 5, 6 MAY 1966

Half acid dream, half latent Lennon laziness personified, 'I'm Only Sleeping' was a joyous celebration of life without pressure. It also conformed to one of the key instructions of the acid trippers, that explorers of the mind should relax and let thoughts come to them, rather than forcing them to appear.

The other-worldly feel of the song was created by artificial means – first speeding up Lennon's vocal to make it sound as if he was singing from beyond the physical plane, and then playing the tape of Harrison's guitar interjections backwards. During the editing process, a fistful of different mixes were prepared, and variations on the basic stereo CD version can be found on vinyl releases scattered around the globe.

LOVE YOU TO

GEORGE HARRISON

RECORDED 11, 13 APRIL 1966

Lester Bangs called it "the first injection of ersatz Eastern wisdom into rock", but George Harrison's translation of the Buddhist spiritual texts he'd been reading in recent months simply reinforced the message of 'Think For Yourself' on the previous album. As far as the public were concerned, though, Harrison had "gone Indian" overnight, an impression reinforced as he took sitar lessons from Ravi Shankar, encouraged the rest of the group to study under the Maharishi Mahesh Yogi, and offered Eastern-sounding songs to the group for the next 18 months.

'Love You To' sounded astonishing alongside the electrifying pop of the 'Revolver' album, where it proved that The Beatles could tackle any genre they wanted. It also inaugurated a less happy tradition, of John Lennon not contributing to the recording of Harrison's songs. One man who did appear, however, was Indian tabla player Anil Bhagwat.

HERE, THERE AND EVERYWHERE

JOHN LENNON/PAUL McCARTNEY

RECORDED 14, 16, 17 JUNE 1966

For the third album running, Paul McCartney turned up with a song that became an instant standard. He credited its original inspiration to multiple hearings of The Beach Boys' 'Pet Sounds' LP, though there's little melodic similarity between them. But the romantic simplicity of the song shone like a beacon through the cynicism and uncertainty that fuelled most of the album.

YELLOW SUBMARINE
JOHN LENNON/PAUL McCARTNEY
RECORDED 26 MAY, 1 JUNE 1966

A simple children's song intended for the equally simple public persona of Ringo Starr, 'Yellow Submarine' still received the full-scale studio treatment. Mark Lewisohn's definitive account of The Beatles' sessions documents

the various effects and gimmicks that were recorded for the song, and then rejected. 'Yellow Submarine' was, in business terms, the most important song on the 'Revolver' LP, as it inspired the cartoon movie which solved the enduring problem of the third film that The Beatles had owed United Artists since the summer of 1965.

SHE SAID SHE SAID
JOHN LENNON/PAUL McCARTNEY
RECORDED 21 JUNE 1966

Another major Lennon song on an album dominated by his paranoid acid visions, 'She Said She Said' was inspired by a doom-laden, LSD-driven remark by actor Peter Fonda, who buttonholed Lennon at a celebrity party with the words "I know what it's like to be dead". 'Tomorrow Never Knows' captured the horror of that statement; 'She Said She Said' turned it into an early piece of Lennon autobiography, the first step on the journey to his 'Plastic Ono Band' album. And all this turmoil and angst was contained within a brilliant three-minute pop song.

GOOD DAY SUNSHINE
JOHN LENNON/PAUL McCARTNEY
RECORDED 8, 9 JUNE 1966

Perfect summer pop for the era, McCartney's 'Good Day Sunshine' had enough melodic twists and turns (note the harmonic shifts in the final chorus) to put it beyond the reach of most would-be cover artists. Simple, effective and stunning, it was the ideal complement to the darker 'Revolver' songs.

AND YOUR BIRD CAN SING
JOHN LENNON/PAUL McCARTNEY
RECORDED 26 APRIL 1966

John Lennon described this song as "another horror", and he wrote it, so he should know. It's full of the fake wisdom of those philosophically lightweight days when it seemed as if the world could be turned on its axis by a tab of acid and a few seconds' thought. Musically, though, it's one of the highlights of the album, powered by a twisting, insidious guitar riff and featuring one of Lennon's most deadpan, off-hand vocals. Rich and mysterious, the track may have been fancy paper round an empty box, but the package sounded so good that no-one cared.

FOR NO ONE
JOHN LENNON/PAUL McCARTNEY
RECORDED 9, 16, 19 MAY 1966

Just two Beatles appeared on McCartney's 'For No One', Ringo playing percussion, and Paul singing and playing keyboards and the lovely descending bass line. The French horn, allowed a lengthy solo in George Martin's score, was performed by Alan Civil from the London Philharmonia. The song itself was another remarkable McCartney ballad, melodically sophisticated and lyrically mature.

DOCTOR ROBERT
JOHN LENNON/PAUL McCARTNEY
RECORDED 17, 19 APRIL 1966

Named without any hint of disguise after a London 'doctor' who could be guaranteed to supply rock stars with exotic drugs on demand, John Lennon's 'Doctor Robert' was hinged around the same rough-edged guitar

as 'And Your Bird Can Sing'. And once again, his lead vocal oozed cynicism and emotional distance, like the world-weary survivor of three years' hard Beatlemania that he was.

I WANT TO TELL YOU
GEORGE HARRISON
RECORDED 2, 3 JUNE 1966

Allowed three songs on any Beatles album for the first time (and also the last, with the exception of the double 'White Album'), George Harrison had the chance to expose several different facets of his songwriting talent. Like 'If I Needed Someone', 'I Want To Tell You' was hinged around The Beatles' superb harmonies (Lennon and McCartney seemed to relish the role of backing singers, relieved of the pressure to carry the song). Once again, Harrison unwrapped an awkward, determinedly realistic view of relationships, in which failed communication was the order of the day. Throughout The Beatles' career, George never wrote a straightforward love song: all his portrayals of romance were surrounded in misunderstanding and the dreadful prospect of boredom, and this was no exception.

GOT TO GET YOU INTO MY LIFE
JOHN LENNON/PAUL McCARTNEY
RECORDED 8, 11 APRIL, 18 MAY, 17 JUNE 1966

'Revolver' revealed The Beatles as master of any musical genre they cared to touch. Having satirised white musicians' desire to play black musical styles in the title of 'Rubber Soul', Paul McCartney turned his hand to the 1966 soul boom with ease, concocting this fabulous piece of mock-Stax, with five brassmen providing the final Memphis-style touches. The hand of control was evident throughout, with the brass sound deliberately 'limited' to create a faintly unreal sound.

Trivia note: compare the fade-outs of the mono and stereo versions of this song, and you'll find entirely different McCartney ad-libs.

TOMORROW NEVER KNOWS
JOHN LENNON/PAUL McCARTNEY
RECORDED 6, 7, 22 APRIL 1966

Almost five months after The Beatles added their final vocals to the charming 'I'm Looking Through You', they were back in the studio – to create three minutes of turmoil that envisaged the death of the conscious mind and the triumph beyond death of the universal spirit. What had happened between November 1965 and April 1966? John Lennon had been on a dual voyage of discovery – experimenting with the hallucogenic powers of LSD, and finding that it was possible to match the chaotic visions he saw on his chemically-fuelled trips with collages of sound.

Both Lennon and McCartney began creating mind movies at their home studios, extended webs of noise that were based around tape loops and 'found sounds'. McCartney was the pioneer in this regard, and it was he who supervised the addition of the almost supernatural squawks and howls that punctuated the song. But the concept was Lennon's, taken from his reading of *The Tibetan Book Of The Dead*. Like Harrison, Lennon noted the similarity between the imagery of Eastern spirituality, and the beyond-consciousness experiences of the acid trip. 'Tomorrow Never Knows', with its eerie 'treated' vocal, droning drums and terrifying soundscape, was the ultimate expression of his discovery – and of the enormous change in The Beatles since they'd finished 'Rubber Soul'

Sgt. Pepper's Lonely Hearts Club Band

PARLOPHONE

CDP7 46442 2

"The biggest influence on 'Sgt. Pepper' was 'Pet Sounds' by The Beach Boys," said Paul McCartney in 1980. "That album just flipped me. When I heard it, I thought, 'Oh dear, this is the album of all time. What the hell are we going to do?' My ideas took off from that standard. I had this idea that it was going to be an album of another band that wasn't us – we'd just imagine all the time that it wasn't us playing. It was just a nice little device to give us some distance on the album. The cover was going to be us dressed as this other band in crazy gear; but it was all stuff that we'd always wanted to wear. And we were going to have photos on the wall of all our heroes." That's the standard view of 'Sgt. Pepper', from the man who almost single-handedly created the album, and its legend. In this reading, 'Pepper' is the best pop record of all time – the album that customarily wins critics' polls, the masterpiece that first persuaded 'serious' musical critics pop was worth their consideration.

There's a rival view of the whole affair, however, and it was put forward most cogently by McCartney's supposed partner, John Lennon. "Paul said 'come and see the show' on that album," he moaned a few years after its release. "I didn't. I had to knock off a few songs so I knocked off 'A Day In The Life', or

my section of it, and 'Mr Kite'. I was very paranoid in those days. I could hardly move."

More than any other Beatles album bar 'Abbey Road', 'Sgt. Pepper' was a Paul McCartney creation. He it was who dreamed up the concept, the title, the idea behind Peter Blake's remarkable cover, the orchestrations, and the device of pretending that the entire LP was the work of another band entirely – which in turn became one of the major themes of the *Yellow Submarine* movie, then in its pre-production stages.

Meanwhile, John Lennon was deep in a creative trough. For the first time, Lennon and McCartney appeared – to Lennon, at least – to be in competition rather than on the same side. Since The Beatles had played their final live shows in August, McCartney had been composing – first the musical themes for the film *The Family Way*, then the songs that would appear on the next Beatles album. Lennon had also been involved in film work, but as an actor, in Dick Lester's *How I Won The War*. Required for the part to shed his Beatle locks, he adopted the granny specs that soon became his trademark, stared into the mirror, and wondered what the future might bring for an unemployed Beatle. Back in England at the end of the filming, Lennon regarded McCartney's enthusiasm to get into the studio as a threat. Aware that he was likely to be outnumbered in the songwriting stakes, he raised the emotional barriers and took against the 'Pepper' album from the start.

In the end, Lennon came up with the requisite number of songs for the album, but he never warmed to the concept. On 'Revolver', and again on the majestic 'Strawberry Fields Forever', cut early in the sessions, he'd experienced the relief and satisfaction of writing from the heart. For 'Pepper', he was back where he'd been in 1964, writing songs to order. Hence the sarcastic, dismissive comments he reserved for this album throughout the rest of his life.

Whatever else 'Sgt. Pepper' may or may not have been, it was certainly an event. It unified British pop culture in a way no other occasion could match. Maybe in hindsight it wasn't The Beatles' strongest album, but it had an impact unlike any record before or since. It literally revolutionised the direction of pop, helping to divide it between those who were prepared to follow the group along the path of experimentation (thus creating 'rock') and those who mourned the loss of the less significant Beatles of yore (the champions of 'pop'). After 'Pepper', nothing was ever the same again – within or without The Beatles.

SGT. PEPPER'S LONELY HEARTS CLUB BAND

JOHN LENNON/PAUL McCARTNEY

RECORDED 1, 2 FEBRUARY, 3, 6 MARCH 1967

Complete with the appropriate sound effects, the album's up-tempo title track introduced the record, the concept and the Club Band. It performed the function of an overture in an opera, preparing the audience for what was to follow, and introducing the themes that supposedly unified the piece.

WITH A LITTLE HELP FROM MY FRIENDS

JOHN LENNON/PAUL McCARTNEY

RECORDED 29, 30 MARCH 1967

Beatles official biographer Hunter Davies watched Lennon, McCartney and their associates completing work on Paul McCartney's original idea, aware from the start that this would be a vehicle for Ringo Starr – or 'Billy Shears', as he was billed in the opening seconds of the song. Though the song's theme was tailored towards Ringo's warm public image (right down to the line "what would you say if I sang out of tune", a real possibility), at

least one observer saw a hidden meaning. Speaking in 1970, US Vice-President Spiro Agnew told an audience that he had recently been informed that the song was a tribute to the power of illegal drugs – news to its composers, perhaps.

Not often did other performers outclass The Beatles with cover versions of their songs, but Joe Cocker's gut-wrenching version of 'Friends' in 1968 left Ringo floundering.

LUCY IN THE SKY WITH DIAMONDS

JOHN LENNON/PAUL McCARTNEY

RECORDED 1, 2 MARCH 1967

The minor furore over the meaning of 'Friends' had nothing on the frenzied response to this piece of whimsy from the pen of John Lennon. "I was consciously writing poetry," he admitted, shifting blame for the line about "newspaper taxis" to his nominal co-writer. But the *Alice In Wonderland* style imagery, supposedly inspired by a drawing John's son Julian had brought home from nursery school, was widely believed to be a description of an acid trip. As soon as someone noticed the initials of the song's title (LSD), that seemed to clinch the story – except that Lennon continued to deny it until his dying day. Having owned up to so much else down the years, there was no reason for him to lie – especially over a song which he always felt was "so badly recorded".

GETTING BETTER
JOHN LENNON/PAUL McCARTNEY
RECORDED 9, 10, 21, 23 MARCH 1967

Based on a favourite saying of Beatles friend/chauffeur Terry Doran, 'Getting Better' was a McCartney song augmented by Lennon, who contributed the self-accusing verse that began "I used to be cruel to my woman". Ever since Lennon's death, McCartney has bemoaned his inability to find a co-writer who, like John, would answer a line like "it's getting better all the time" with "can't get much worse". Even in the midst of what was intended to be a concept album, McCartney could turn out a song that was clever, melodic, memorable and universal in its application.

FIXING A HOLE
JOHN LENNON/PAUL McCARTNEY
RECORDED 9, 21 FEBRUARY 1967

For the first time in England, The Beatles left Abbey Road studios for the session that provided the basic track for this fine McCartney song, often overlooked by critics and fans alike. EMI's studio was fully booked for the night, so the group moved to Regent Sound in the West End, where The Rolling Stones' early hits had been taped.

While John Lennon's writing veered between fantasy and obvious self-revelation, McCartney's skirted from the romantic to the delightfully oblique. This song definitely fell into the latter category, with lyrics that unveiled as many mysteries as they solved. Instrumentally, too, 'Fixing A Hole' was a minor classic, from McCartney's opening trills on the harpsichord to Harrison's lyrical guitar solo.

SHE'S LEAVING HOME
JOHN LENNON/PAUL McCARTNEY
RECORDED 17, 20 MARCH 1967

"Paul had the basic theme for this song," said John Lennon, "but all those lines like 'We sacrificed most of our life... We gave her everything that money could buy', those were the things Mimi used to say to me. It was easy to write." Paul's rather precious piece of fictional writing wasn't helped by Mike Leander's ornate score for the song, one of the few occasions when The Beatles were left sounding pretentious. It took the realism of Lennon's answer-lines to cut through the sweetness of the piece.

BEING FOR THE BENEFIT OF MR. KITE

JOHN LENNON/PAUL McCARTNEY

RECORDED 17, 20 FEBRUARY, 28, 29, 31 MARCH 1967

A masterpiece of ingenuity rather than inspiration, 'Mr Kite' was written when John transcribed the wording from a vintage circus poster into verse form, and recorded with the help of scores of small segments of fairground organ tape, tossed into the air and then stuck back together to produce the eerie noise that dominates the instrumental sections. Lennon dismissed it as a throwaway – which, when you remember how it was made, is pretty apt.

WITHIN YOU WITHOUT YOU

GEORGE HARRISON

RECORDED 15, 22 MARCH, 3, 4 APRIL 1967

Though it was John Lennon who resented Paul McCartney's domination of the 'Pepper' sessions, George Harrison probably had more cause to be aggrieved. He was restricted to just one number on the LP, his other contribution ('Only A Northern Song') being rejected.

Like 'Love You To', 'Within You, Without You' blatantly displayed George's infatuation with Indian culture. Recorded with the assistance of several Indian musicians, plus Beatles aide Neil Aspinall on tamboura, the song required no help from any other member of the group. "It was written at Klaus Voorman's house in Hampstead, one night after dinner," George explained a decade later. "I was playing a pedal harmonium when it came, the tune first, then the first sentence." Some thought it a masterpiece, some a prime example of mock-philosophical babble. Either way, it was pure Harrison.

WHEN I'M SIXTY-FOUR
JOHN LENNON/PAUL McCARTNEY
RECORDED 6, 8, 20, 21 DECEMBER 1966

Paul began writing this song when he was a teenager, needing only to add the middle sections for this revival of a ten-year-old melody. Within the concept of the album, it fitted the image of the Edwardian Pepper band, whereas it would have seemed mawkish on any of the group's earlier LPs. The addition of clarinets to the mix heightened the pre-First World War feel.

LOVELY RITA
JOHN LENNON/PAUL McCARTNEY
RECORDED 23, 24 FEBRUARY, 7, 21 MARCH 1967\

The anthem for traffic wardens ("meter maids") everywhere, 'Lovely Rita' was a glorious throwaway, full of musical jokes and brimming with self-confidence. Nothing on the record expressed that as fully as the piano solo, ironically played by keyboard maestro George Martin.

GOOD MORNING, GOOD MORNING
JOHN LENNON/PAUL McCARTNEY
RECORDED 8, 16 FEBRUARY, 13, 28, 29 MARCH 1967

Using a TV commercial for Kellogg's cereal as his starting point, John Lennon concocted a wonderfully dry satire on contemporary urban life. Several points to watch out for here: the reference to the popular BBC TV sitcom, *Meet The Wife*; the ultra-compressed brass sound provided by members of Sounds Incorporated; a stinging Harrison guitar solo; and the cavalcade of animals, in ascending order of ferocity, which segues into the next track.

SGT. PEPPER'S LONELY HEARTS CLUB BAND (REPRISE)
JOHN LENNON/PAUL McCARTNEY
RECORDED 1 APRIL 1967

For the first but definitely not last time, Paul McCartney topped and tailed a set of songs by reprising the opening melody, in true Hollywood musical fashion.

A DAY IN THE LIFE

JOHN LENNON/PAUL McCARTNEY

RECORDED 19, 20 JANUARY, 3,10,22 FEBRUARY, 21 APRIL 1967

Delete 'A Day In The Life' from 'Sgt. Pepper' and you'd have an elegant, playful album of pop songs. With it, the LP assumes some kind of greatness. Some might vote for 'Hey Jude' or 'Strawberry Fields Forever' as the finest ever Beatles recording, but 'A Day In The Life' would run anything close – and it's certainly the best ever collaborative effort between Lennon and McCartney.

Lennon wrote the basic song, its verses a snapshot from his own life and the world around him – the death of a friend in a car crash, a newspaper cutting about the state of the roads in Blackburn, Lancashire. The tag line "I'd love to turn you on" brought a broadcasting ban in Britain: more importantly, it led twice into an overwhelming orchestral assault, with 40 musicians headed helter-skelter up the scales towards a crescendo of silence. First time around, the barrage leads into McCartney's stoned middle-eight, another day in another life; second time, there's a pause, and then a piano chord that resounds for almost a minute. Then bathos: a whistle only dogs could hear, followed by the locked-groove gibberish that brought the side to a close, and is sampled briefly at the end of the CD. Stunning, magnificent, awesome: there's nothing in rock to match it.

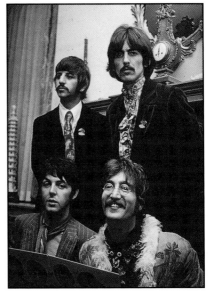

Magical Mystery Tour

The Fool On The Hill Flying Blue Jay Way
Your Mother Should Know I Am The Walrus

BEATLES

MAGICAL MYSTERY TOUR

Hello Goodbye Strawberry Fields Forever
Penny Lane Baby You're A Rich Man
All You Need Is Love

Magical Mystery Tour

PARLOPHONE

CDP7 48062 2

Early in April 1967, with 'Sgt. Pepper' not yet complete, Paul McCartney flew to America for a week's holiday. On his return flight, he drafted out his idea for a TV special which would involve a mystery tour on a coach – not the usual British seaside trip to a less than exotic location twenty miles down the coast, but a voyage into the imagination. By mid-April, McCartney had written the title tune for the project, and the four Beatles had agreed a tentative format for the programme. What with the intervention of the Maharishi Mahesh Yogi, and the unexpected death of Brian Epstein, the project wasn't completed until almost the end of the year. When it was ready for public screening, it was scheduled for prime-time viewing on BBC TV, as part of the programming for Boxing Day 1967. Used to a stodgy diet of sitcoms and variety shows, the great British public responded to the frequently bizarre and often amateurish Magical Mystery Tour with bewilderment bordering on anger. The professional reviewers were equally damning, and the film passed into history as The Beatles' first major flirtation with public disapproval.

The reasons for the failure were varied. The film was originally shown in black-and-white, thereby losing the visual impact of many of the sequences. The public hadn't known what to expect, and many viewers were assuming that the show would be the kind of song-and-dance spectacular that the closing 'Your Mother Should Know' sequence satirised. Mostly, though, the criticisms were justified. For all its brilliant set pieces, *Magical Mystery Tour* desperately required professional editing and direction. Self-indulgent and unrestrained, it showed The Beatles that they didn't have an automatic lock on the public's taste.

As usual with a McCartney idea post-1966, John Lennon felt resentful about the entire project. "Paul had a tendency to come along and say, well, he's written his ten songs, let's record now," he moaned in 1970. "And I said, well, give us a few days and I'll knock a few off. He set *Magical Mystery Tour* up and had worked it out with (*Beatles roadie*) Mal Evans, and then he came and showed me what his idea was, the story and how he had it all, the production and everything. George and I were sort of grumbling, you know, 'Fuckin' movie, oh well, we better do it'."

Six new songs were written and recorded for the film. The Beatles finally elected to release them as a double-EP package, at twice normal single price, complete with a cartoon book vaguely telling the story of the film. The American market wasn't geared up for EPs, however, so Capitol turned the two EPs into an LP, adding in the earlier Beatles singles from 1967. In that format, the album was heavily imported into Britain, and eventually won a full release here in the late Seventies. When EMI prepared The Beatles' albums for CD, 'Magical Mystery Tour' automatically took its place in the line-up, between 'Pepper' and 'The White Album'.

MAGICAL MYSTERY TOUR
JOHN LENNON/PAUL McCARTNEY

RECORDED 25, 26, 27 APRIL, 3 MAY, 7 NOVEMBER 1967

Aside from some vocal additions in November, the title track from the *Magical Mystery Tour* film was completed before 'Sgt. Pepper' was released. It was a McCartney effort from start to finish, embellished by the use of session brass players, and with Paul himself acting as a carnival barker at the start to drag the punters in.

No fewer than three different versions of the track were made available to the public at the end of 1967. The film mix remains unavailable on record, but both the mono and stereo versions were included when EMI issued a boxed set of The Beatles' EPs on compact disc. The CD album, meanwhile, has the stereo version.

THE FOOL ON THE HILL
JOHN LENNON/PAUL McCARTNEY

RECORDED 25, 26, 27 SEPTEMBER, 20, 25 OCTOBER 1967

Maintaining his record of writing an instant standard on every mid-Sixties Beatles album, Paul McCartney composed this touching, beautiful ballad late in the proceedings, cutting a solo demo at the piano, and then concocting a deliciously light and airy arrangement for the final version. Three flute players added to the atmosphere (once again the mono and stereo mixes differ, most notably in their placement of the flute interjections).

FLYING
JOHN LENNON/PAUL McCARTNEY
GEORGE HARRISON/RICHARD STARKEY
RECORDED 8, 28 SEPTEMBER 1967

No other Beatles recording underwent such drastic editing as this instrumental with vocal backing. Intended to support a psychedelic section of the film, rich in shifts of colour and texture, it was suitably eerie – and bizarre, apparently ending with a jazz section borrowed from elsewhere in The Beatles' collective record library. All that was removed as the track was sliced from ten minutes to little more than two, leaving 'Flying' as an off-the-wall EP-filler — the only instrumental The Beatles issued on EMI, and also their first four-man composition.

BLUE JAY WAY
GEORGE HARRISON
RECORDED 6, 7 SEPTEMBER, 6 OCTOBER 1967

George Harrison was at his rented home on Blue Jay Way in Los Angeles, waiting for former Beatle aide Derek Taylor to arrive for dinner. Taylor, fortuitously, was late, and Harrison turned his mild concern and irritation into this song. What could have been a simple, maudlin ditty was transformed by The Beatles' studio prowess into an exotic, almost mystical journey. Harrison's vocal was treated until it sounded as if it was coming from beyond the grave, though with none of the ghostly threat of Lennon's similarly altered voice on 'Tomorrow Never Knows'. Backwards tapes, droning organs, and a cello combined to heighten the Eastern atmosphere – without a single Indian instrument being employed.

YOUR MOTHER SHOULD KNOW
JOHN LENNON/PAUL McCARTNEY
RECORDED 22, 23 AUGUST, 29 SEPTEMBER 1967

Simple and nostalgic alongside the calculated experimentation of the other film soundtrack songs, 'Your Mother Should Know' inspired one of the great *Magical Mystery Tour* set pieces, as The Beatles waltzed down a huge staircase in white suits, like refugees from a 1930s Hollywood musical.

I AM THE WALRUS
JOHN LENNON/PAUL McCARTNEY
RECORDED 5, 6, 27, 28, 29 SEPTEMBER 1967

"I was the Walrus, whatever that means. The Walrus was a big capitalist that are all the fucking oysters, if you must know. I always had this image of the Walrus in the garden and I loved it, so I didn't ever check out what the Walrus was. But he's a fucking bastard, that's what he turns out to be. Everybody presumes that means something, that just because I said I am the Walrus, it must mean I am God or something, but it's just poetry."

That's John Lennon in 1970, attempting to debunk all the theories that had been inspired by the oblique lyrical stance of his sole contribution to the *Magical Mystery Tour* soundtrack. He revealed many years later that 'Walrus' had been a deliberate effort to mystify his critics and followers alike, by stringing together violently dissimilar images without a shred of continuity.

Lennon enjoyed watching the outside world interpreting his nonsense verse, and relished the recording of the song, which – like 'Blue Jay Way' – became the vehicle for another bout of studio experimentation. (As was often the case with The Beatles' most unusual recordings, several slightly different mixes of 'Walrus' were issued around the world.)

Among the delights on offer were a mellotron, heavily used by Lennon at home and in the studio in 1967; a 12-piece string section; 16 members of the Mike Sammes Singers, chanting "Oompah, oompah, stick it up your number"; and several lines of Shakespeare's *King Lear*, lifted from a BBC radio drama production being broadcast during the mixing session.

HELLO GOODBYE
JOHN LENNON/PAUL McCARTNEY
RECORDED 2, 19, 20, 25 OCTOBER, 2 NOVEMBER 1967

To John Lennon's disgust, his epic 'I Am The Walrus' was issued on the flipside of this commercial but rather inconsequential McCartney composition – three minutes of contradictions and meaningless juxtapositions, with a tune that was impossible to forget. More interesting than the song were The Beatles' four promotional films, shot at London's Saville Theatre, none of which was able to be shown on British TV at the time because of Union rules about miming.

STRAWBERRY FIELDS FOREVER

JOHN LENNON/PAUL McCARTNEY

RECORDED 29 NOVEMBER, 8, 9, 10, 21, 22 DECEMBER 1966

The greatest pop record ever made? Almost certainly it is, though it shares with its partner, 'Penny Lane', the less glorious fate of having broken a run of Beatles No. 1 hits that went all the way back to 'Please Please Me' four years earlier. In what is arguably the most disgraceful statistic in chart history and to the eternal shame of the British record buying public, Engelbert Humperdinck's vacuous ballad 'Release Me' prevented The Beatles' double sided slab of genius from reaching the top.

Ostensibly inspired by a Liverpool children's home familiar from his boyhood, 'Strawberry Fields Forever' was actually an attempt by John Lennon to chart the process of consciousness and understanding, through fragmented lyrical images. The story behind the finished record is familiar: two different renditions of the song, in entirely different moods and keys, were cleverly edited together by George Martin via the use of variable tape-speed. If ever a song deserved such serendipity, it was this one – a record that never dates, because it lives outside time.

PENNY LANE

JOHN LENNON/PAUL McCARTNEY

RECORDED 29, 30 DECEMBER 1966, 4, 6, 9, 10, 12, 17 JANUARY 1967

"'Penny Lane'/'Strawberry Fields Forever' was the best record we ever made," reckoned Beatles producer George Martin. McCartney's nostalgic 'Penny Lane' didn't have the psychic tension of Lennon's 'Strawbery Fields', but it was every bit as imaginative and lyrical. No other single displays the complementary talents of the Lennon/McCartney pairing so well.

While John's song was locked in the mind, Paul's roamed the streets of Liverpool with a smile on its face. The music matched that

sense of freedom, with the crowning touch supplied by David Mason's piccolo trumpet solo. A closing Mason flourish was removed from the song in the final mix, though only after an early mix had been sent to the States, for use on promo copies of the single.

BABY YOU'RE A RICH MAN
JOHN LENNON/PAUL McCARTNEY
RECORDED 11 MAY 1967

"We just stuck two songs together for this one," admitted John Lennon, "the same as 'A Day In The Life'." The final effect wasn't quite as grandiose, but 'Baby You're A Rich Man' certainly took less time to record – being started and finished in a single six-hour session. Rumours that the song's final choruses contain a hidden 'tribute' to Brian Epstein – "baby you're a rich fag Jew" – appear to be groundless. But it is true that the number was originally intended for the *Yellow Submarine* soundtrack, though it ended up being released a year before the film on the flipside of 'All You Need Is Love'. The instrument punctuating the song that sounds like a manic trumpet is a primitive synthesiser called a Clavioline, incidentally.

ALL YOU NEED IS LOVE
JOHN LENNON/PAUL McCARTNEY
RECORDED 14, 19, 23, 24, 25 JUNE 1967

In 1967, satellite technology finally allowed instant visual communication between every corner of the globe. To celebrate this achievement, international broadcasting organisations united to stage *Our World*, a programme which would bring together segments from every continent, as part of a multinational live TV show.

The Beatles were invited to contribute to the British section of the show, performing a new song. With universal appeal in mind, John Lennon wrote 'All You Need Is Love', one of the anthems of the Sixties. The decision was made to broadcast the actual recording of the song live – or so the public were informed, though Lennon and the other Beatles sang and played along to a pre-recorded backing track, and John actually re-cut his lead vocal a few hours later. The broadcast passed without incident, and remains one of the strongest visual impressions of the summer of love, as a mini-orchestra and many of the group's friends from the pop aristocracy congregated in the cavernous Studio One at Abbey Road.

The BEATLES

The Beatles
(The White Album)

PARLOPHONE

CDS7 46443 8

On one hand, 'The Beatles' – 'The White Album', as all but pedants call it – was the most diverse record that The Beatles, or probably any pop band in history, has ever made. On the other, as Paul McCartney remembered, "That was the tension album. We were all in the midst of that psychedelic thing, or just coming out of it. In any case, it was weird. Never before had we recorded with beds in the studio and people visiting for hours on end: business meetings and all that. There was a lot of friction during that album. We were just about to break up, and that was tense in itself." Lester Bangs described it perfectly: "The first album by The Beatles or in the history of rock by four solo artists in one band". In doing that, he was simply following John Lennon's lead: "If you took each track, it was just me and a backing group, Paul and a backing group – I enjoyed it, but we broke up then."

During the course of the sessions, Ringo Starr actually quit the group for more than a week, before ambling back when he realised that the others were continuing the album without him. Ringo is unlikely to have been at the centre of the dissension in the ranks: the main arguments were between George and Paul (Harrison reckoning that McCartney was treating him as a junior member of the band) and John and the rest of the band (over, on one side, Lennon's insistence on Yoko Ono joining the group in the studio and, on the other, her treatment at the hands of Paul and George).

There were plenty of other pressures at work. The lack of central management in the group's career since the death of Brian Epstein in August 1967 had presented them with additional financial and business decisions to worry about, ignore and occasionally even make. McCartney's keen interest in maintaining a steady ship rubbed up against Lennon and Harrison's more *laissez-faire* attitude to events.

The creation of Apple, their multi-genre business empire that was intended as a fantasy come true but rapidly disintegrated into chaos, took its toll on the group's unity and enthusiasm. So too did the aftermath of the Maharishi episode, with even the most meditation-friendly of The Beatles suffering extreme disillusionment after their idyll with the Indian guru mutated into farce. Most of all, though, the group were individually and collectively aware that without leadership or a definite direction, they had no unifying purpose. From the start of 1968 onwards, they seemed to work to a 'two steps forward, three steps back, one step into another dimension' policy – with results that were often inspired, and just as often muddle-headed.

It's some kind of proof of their genius, then, that 'The White Album' was so brilliant, and so vast. Producer George Martin always wanted the group to throw away the chaff and trim the 30-track, 90-minute epic into a tight 40-minute LP of polished gems. But half the attraction of 'The White Album' is its sprawling chaos. Such a giant canvas allowed The Beatles, more often one at a time than not, to show off every aspect of their music. For the first and probably last time in pop history, a group demonstrated on one release that they could handle rock'n'roll, reggae, soul, blues, folk, country, pop and even the avant-garde with consummate ease – and still come out sounding like The Beatles. As a handy history of popular music since 1920, or simply a rich mine of battered gems, 'The Beatles' is impossible to beat.

For the last time, both mono and stereo mixes of this double-album were prepared, and The Beatles took great delight in making them as different from each other as possible. Almost every song on 'The White Album' has variations between the two mixes: in one extreme case, the mono version is 20 seconds shorter than the stereo.

BACK IN THE USSR
JOHN LENÑON/PAUL McCARTNEY
RECORDED 22, 23 AUGUST 1968

For many of the 'White Album' sessions, The Beatles were able to work on separate, individual projects at the same time, and keep their four-man performances – and the resulting tension they caused – to a minimum. But on August 22nd 1968, when all of The Beatles assembled to record Paul McCartney's 'Back In The USSR', tempers frayed, and it was Ringo Starr – pegged by the world as the least opinioned of the group – who walked out, announcing he'd quit the band.

In his place, McCartney played drums, with a little assistance from Lennon and Harrison; and the entire song was cut without Ringo. The result was a magnificent Beach Boys pastiche, which that group's lead singer, Mike Love, later claimed to have helped write. Hunter Davies's official Beatles biography, published in 1968, offered another story.

DEAR PRUDENCE
JOHN LENNON/PAUL McCARTNEY
RECORDED 28, 29, 30 AUGUST 1968

Prudence Farrow, sister of the actress Mia, was the subject of this generous, warm-hearted Lennon song. It was inspired by her behaviour at the Maharishi's Indian retreat, when Lennon was deputed to entice her out of her self-enforced hiding in her quarters. Lennon widened the song to take in a pantheistic vision of the world's beauty, one of the few positive statements to emerge from his stay in India. (Another, a song called 'Child Of Nature', wasn't considered for this album; instead, it was rewritten three years later as 'Jealous Guy' for the 'Imagine' LP, its original spirit of universal harmony replaced by fear and guilt.)

This was another of the recordings done during Ringo Starr's departure from the group: strange that The Beatles should open their album with two tracks that were both recorded by a three-man line-up.

GLASS ONION
JOHN LENNON/PAUL McCARTNEY
RECORDED 11, 12, 13, 16 SEPTEMBER, 10 OCTOBER 1968

Like 'I Am The Walrus', 'Glass Onion' was written by John Lennon as a deliberate riposte to critics and fans who thought they were discovering the Holy Grail in some of his more recherché lyrical imagery. "I wrote 'The Walrus was Paul' in that song," John explained many years later. "At that time I was still in my love cloud with Yoko, so I thought I'd just say something nice to Paul – you did a good job over these few years, holding us together. I thought, I've got Yoko, and you can have the credit."

Besides the deliberately obtuse lyrics 'Glass Onion' boasted a searing Lennon vocal, and a mournful string coda that cut against the mood of the song.

OB-LA-DI, OB-LA-DA
JOHN LENNON/PAUL McCARTNEY
RECORDED 3, 4, 5, 8, 9, 11, 15 JULY 1968

Day after day, Paul McCartney dragged The Beatles through take after take, and arrangement after arrangement, of a throwaway, mock-reggae tune about a singer and a man who "has a barrow in the marketplace". Was it worth it? Well, the song has humour on its side, especially with the other Beatles throwing in the off-the-cuff comments that were fast becoming a trademark on their 1968 recordings. And 'Ob-La-Di, Ob-La-Da' did become a No. 1 hit for Marmalade. But rarely in The Beatles' career did they spend so much time on something so ephemeral.

WILD HONEY PIE
JOHN LENNON/PAUL McCARTNEY
RECORDED 20 AUGUST 1968

During the 'White Album' sessions, Paul McCartney felt comfortable enough for the first time to capture some of his one-minute moments of madness on tape. He recorded this strange, whimsical ditty as a one-man band, overdubbing several vocal parts and guitars, and emerging with 53 seconds of music that would never have been considered for release on any Beatles album but this one.

THE CONTINUING STORY OF BUNGALOW BILL
JOHN LENNON/PAUL McCARTNEY
RECORDED 8 OCTOBER 1968

Anything went for this one-day session – a Spanish guitar intro borrowed from a sound effects tape, a vocal cameo from Yoko Ono, harmonies from Ringo's wife, Maureen Starkey, and mellotron from producer Chris Thomas. Lennon's lyrics told the semi-humorous story of a fellow Meditation convert, addicted to big game hunting, and everyone in the vicinity of the studio contributed to the singalong chorus.

WHILE MY GUITAR GENTLY WEEPS
GEORGE HARRISON
RECORDED 5, 6 SEPTEMBER 1968

George Harrison won such acclaim for this song that he was tempted to write a much less successful follow-up, 'This Guitar (Can't Keep From Crying)'. Ironically, the most famous guitar solo on any Beatles record was played by an outsider – Cream guitarist Eric Clapton, a close friend of Harrison's, who was invited to the session both for his musical skills and in an attempt to cool the frequently heated passions in the studio.

As it was originally written, and demoed via a solo performance at Abbey Road, Harrison's song had an additional verse, which didn't survive beyond this initial (and quite magical) acoustic performance.

HAPPINESS IS A WARM GUN
JOHN LENNON/PAUL McCARTNEY
RECORDED 24, 25 SEPTEMBER 1968

The song's original title – 'Happiness Is A Warm Gun In Your Hand' – left its social message perfectly clear. But besides reflecting John Lennon's moral outrage at the American firearms lobby, it also had a second function, as John explained: "It's sort of a history of rock and roll." And a third inspiration for the track was confirmed later, when he revealed that much of the most direct imagery in the song conveyed his sexual passion for Yoko Ono. Beatles and Apple Corps press officer Derek Taylor contributed some of the song's most mysterious lines.

Musically, the track was a *tour de force*, albeit without the theatrics and orchestrations of the

'Pepper' album. It moved swiftly from a dream state to an air of menace, then a frenetic middle section, and finally a repeated four-chord chorus which somehow combined erotic fervour with an affectionate pastiche of 50s rock'n'roll.

MARTHA MY DEAR
JOHN LENNON/PAUL McCARTNEY
RECORDED 4, 5 OCTOBER 1968

What began as a McCartney solo piece, a deliciously romantic piano piece in his utterly distinctive style, ended up with the accompaniment augmented by a troupe of brass and string musicians. Thankfully, they didn't bury the whimsical charm of the song, whose heroine took her name from McCartney's near-legendary sheepdog.

I'M SO TIRED
JOHN LENNON/PAUL McCARTNEY
RECORDED 8 OCTOBER 1968

Like 'Yer Blues', 'I'm So Tired' wins the Lennon prize for irony, this paean of self-doubt and boredom having been composed in the supposedly spiritual surroundings of the

Maharishi Mahesh Yogi's Indian retreat. The ennui and desolation of Lennon's vocal filled in the tiny fragments of obliqueness in one of his most direct songs, and made for an eerie counterpoint to the optimistic, joyous McCartney numbers which surrounded it.

BLACKBIRD
JOHN LENNON/PAUL McCARTNEY
RECORDED 11 JUNE 1968

Nature song? Love ballad? Message of support for the black power movement? McCartney's gently beautiful 'Blackbird' supported several interpretations, but required nothing more than appreciation for its flowing melody and its stark visual imagery. The recording was a solo performance, aided only by bird sounds borrowed from the EMI tape library. Paul never wrote a simpler or more effective song.

PIGGIES
GEORGE HARRISON
RECORDED 19, 20 SEPTEMBER, 10 OCTOBER 1968

With the aid of his mother, who wrote the "damn good whacking" line, George intended

'Piggies' as humorous social satire – though its title soon meant that the counter-culture adopted it as an anti-police anthem. Continuing the animal theme of 'Blackbird', pig noises were added to the basic track (Lennon's sole contribution to the song), which was also augmented by a hefty orchestral arrangement, and a harpsichord played by the man who produced several 'White Album' sessions, Chris Thomas.

ROCKY RACCOON
JOHN LENNON/PAUL McCARTNEY
RECORDED 15 AUGUST 1968

Anyone scouring The Beatles' catalogue for early signs of the playfulness in which Paul McCartney indulged – some would say over-indulged — during his solo career could find plenty of evidence on the 'White Album'. With the assistance of George Martin on saloon-bar piano, the group (minus Harrison) completed this attractive but lightweight mock-Western ditty in just one session.

DON'T PASS ME BY
RICHARD STARKEY
RECORDED 5, 6 JUNE, 12, 22 JULY 1968

After five years of trying, Ringo Starr finally got his first solo composition on a Beatles album. It turned out to be a country hoedown with playful lyrics and a generally lugubrious air, with some off-the-cuff fiddle playing by Jack Fallon, who'd met The Beatles six years earlier when he promoted one of their concerts in Stroud.

For some reason – maybe because they felt it was one of the least important songs on the album – Lennon and McCartney chose to experiment with the mixing of this track, emerging with mono and stereo versions that run at recognisably different speeds, and have variations in the instrumental overdubs.

WHY DON'T WE DO IT IN THE ROAD?
JOHN LENNON/PAUL McCARTNEY
RECORDED 9, 10 OCTOBER 1968

John Lennon called this near-solo McCartney performance "one of his best", which was either sarcasm or showed that he always valued his partner's off-the-cuff moments more than his controlled ones. Ringo added his drums to a basic piano, guitar and vocal track that Paul had recorded without the assistance or knowledge of the other group members. Raucous and good-humoured, it was a rare moment of levity from the man increasingly left to direct the group's activities.

The song's (very) slightly risqué lyric, all two lines of it, heightened the vague air of controversy surrounding the album. McCartney was already in trouble with the press for allowing a minuscule nude picture of himself to be included on the set's free poster.

I WILL
JOHN LENNON/PAUL McCARTNEY
RECORDED 16, 17 SEPTEMBER 1968

It took 67 takes for Lennon, McCartney and Starr to come up with a basic track for this gentle love song which met its composer's expectations. McCartney then added his tuneful vocal, sang his bass part rather than playing it, and still found time during the session to ad-lib a dreamy song called something like 'Can You Take Me Back', which duly found its way onto

the finished album as an uncredited snippet between 'Cry Baby Cry' and 'Revolution 9'.

JULIA
JOHN LENNON/PAUL McCARTNEY
RECORDED 13 OCTOBER 1968

It was Donovan who taught John Lennon the finger-picking style that he used on this song, as well as 1969 recordings like 'Sun King' and Yoko Ono's 'Remember Love'. For the first and last time in The Beatles' career, this was an entirely solo performance by John – dedicated both to his late mother (Julia Lennon) and to Yoko. Translated into English, her name apparently means 'Ocean child', a phrase which was incorporated into Lennon's lyric.

BIRTHDAY
JOHN LENNON/PAUL McCARTNEY
RECORDED 18 SEPTEMBER 1968

Either side of repairing to McCartney's house to watch the classic rock'n'roll movie, 'The Girl Can't Help It', on TV, The Beatles recorded this riff-based rocker – one of the last genuine Lennon/McCartney collaborations. Two Beatle partners, Pattie Harrison and Yoko Ono, sang the answer vocals in the chorus, while the band rocked out as if they hadn't a care in the world. It was a rare show of old-style unity during a difficult few months of recording.

YER BLUES
JOHN LENNON/PAUL McCARTNEY
RECORDED 13, 14, 20 AUGUST 1968

Written from the supposed haven of the Maharishi's camp in Rishikesh, 'Yer Blues' was an anguished confession of loneliness and pain, wrapped in a deliberately self-mocking title. "There was a self-consciousness about suddenly singing blues," Lennon explained in 1970. "I was self-conscious about doing it."

With its references to Bob Dylan and rock'n'roll, 'Yer Blues' was obviously intended to be a definitive statement of Lennon's boredom with his role – definitive, that is, until the "I don't believe in Beatles" cry in 'God' on his 'Plastic Ono Band' album. The song meant enough to him to be reprised both at The Rolling Stones' *Rock'N'Roll Circus* TV show

in December, and at the Toronto festival the following year.

MOTHER NATURE'S SON
JOHN LENNON/PAUL McCARTNEY
RECORDED 9, 20 AUGUST 1968

Like 'Blackbird', 'Mother Nature's Son' was a gentle, pastoral acoustic song which captured McCartney's writing at its most inspired. Augmented by a subtle horn arrangement, it epitomised the devastating switch of moods and tempos that made this album – and indeed The Beatles' work in general – so remarkable.

EVERYBODY'S GOT SOME-THING TO HIDE EXCEPT ME AND MY MONKEY
JOHN LENNON/PAUL McCARTNEY
RECORDED 26, 27 JUNE, 1, 23 JULY 1968

Playing with lyrical opposites, then lapsing into nonsense for the chorus, John Lennon concocted a rock'n'roll song that suggested more than it meant. Such a tongue-in-cheek number deserved an appropriate arrangement, and The Beatles set out to enjoy the process of recording it – speeding up the tape of the backing track to heighten the frantic feel, and then hurling a motley collection of screams, cries and even some singing into the fade-out.

brilliant piano playing, and some acerbic singing from John. Eight bars of instrumental work were removed from the fade-out during the final mix, incidentally.

SEXY SADIE
JOHN LENNON/PAUL McCARTNEY
RECORDED 13, 21 AUGUST 1968

"That was about the Maharishi," explained John in 1970, when quizzed about the identity of the mysterious Ms Sadie. "I copped out and wouldn't write 'Maharishi, what have you done, you made a fool of everyone'. There was a big hullabaloo about him trying to rape Mia Farrow, and things like that. So we went to see him. I was the spokesman, as usual whenever the dirty work came. I said, 'We're leaving'. He asked, 'Why?', and all that shit, and I said, 'Well, if you're so cosmic, you'll know why'."

In the studio, Lennon briefly demonstrated the song's obscene original lyrics, which made no attempt to shield the Maharishi by the use of poetry. On the record, though, the insult was softened by the sheer beauty of the music, which hinged around McCartney's

HELTER SKELTER
JOHN LENNON/PAUL McCARTNEY
RECORDED 9, 10 SEPTEMBER 1968

"That came about because I read in *Melody Maker* that The Who had made some track or other that was the loudest, most raucous rock'n'roll, the dirtiest thing they've ever done," Paul McCartney explained. "I didn't know what track they were talking about but it made me think, 'Right. Got to do it.' And I totally got off on that one little sentence in the paper."

On July 18, then, The Beatles gathered at Abbey Road to match that description, and emerged with a 27-minute jam around a menacing guitar riff. Still unreleased, this live-in-the-studio recording was the heaviest track The Beatles ever made.

Seven weeks later, they tried again, this time aware that they needed to make their statement in five minutes, not 27. Having cut the basic track, they added a chaotic barrage of horns, distortion and guitar feedback, and then prepared two entirely different mixes of the song – the stereo one running almost a minute longer than the mono, which omitted Ringo's pained shout, "I've got blisters on my fingers".

A year later, Charles Manson's followers wrote the words 'Helter Skelter' in blood as they killed actress Sharon Tate and her friends in her Hollywood home. Bizarrely, John Lennon (rather than McCartney, the song's composer) was called as a witness in the trial, but refused to attend. "What's 'Helter Skelter' got to do with knifing somebody?" he complained. "I've never listened to the words properly, it was just a noise."

LONG LONG LONG
GEORGE HARRISON
RECORDED 7, 8, 9 OCTOBER 1968

Without John Lennon, who as usual was mysteriously absent when a Harrison song appeared on the agenda, The Beatles managed 67 takes of this delicately lyrical number. Then they capped a low-key, almost inaudible

performance with a few moments of chaos – capturing the sound of a wine bottle vibrating on top of a speaker cabinet, and matching it with a flurry of guitars, groans and drums.

REVOLUTION 1
JOHN LENNON/PAUL McCARTNEY
RECORDED 30, 31 MAY, 4, 21 JUNE 1968

For the first and last time, The Beatles succeeded on 30 May 1968 in recording the basic backing for two different tracks at exactly the same time. How? It was quite simple. At the first session for their new album, they recorded a ten-minute rendition of John's latest song – best interpreted as an overt political statement, backing the stance of the main Communist Parties in the debates over the student riots in Paris, rather than the calls from ultra-left parties for immediate revolution. (Later, Lennon would take entirely the opposite political position.)

The first four minutes became 'Revolution 1', originally planned as a single but eventually deemed too low-key, and subsequently re-recorded in an entirely electric arrangement; the last six minutes, a cacophony of feedback and vocal improvisation, was transported to become the basis of 'Revolution 9'.

HONEY PIE
JOHN LENNON/PAUL McCARTNEY
RECORDED 1, 2, 4 OCTOBER 1968

Not a revival of a flappers' favourite from the 1920s but a McCartney original, 'Honey Pie' must have owed something to the music of his father Jim McCartney's jazz band. Scratches from an old 78rpm record were added to one of the opening lines of the song, to boost its period flavour. George Martin scored the brass and woodwind arrangement, and that arch experimentalist, John Lennon, was quite happy to add electric guitar to a song that was the total opposite of all his contributions to the album.

SAVOY TRUFFLE
GEORGE HARRISON
RECORDED 3, 5, 11, 14 OCTOBER 1968

George Harrison wrote this playful song, inspired by a close friend: "Eric Clapton had a lot of cavities in his teeth and needed dental

work. He ate a lot of chocolates – he couldn't resist them. I got stuck with the two bridges for a while, and Derek Taylor wrote some of the words in the middle." Taylor therefore collected his second anonymous credit on the 'White Album', but no royalties. Harrison, meanwhile, borrowed most of the lyrics from the inside of a chocolate box, while John Lennon commented on proceedings by not turning up for any of the sessions where the song was recorded.

CRY BABY CRY
JOHN LENNON/PAUL McCARTNEY
RECORDED 16, 18 JULY 1968

Consult Hunter Davies's book once again to find John Lennon's rather apologetic description of how he wrote this song – which in one of his final interviews he denied ever having been involved with, the two days of sessions obviously struck from his mental record.

Using characters that sounded as if they'd been borrowed from a Lewis Carroll story, Lennon spent some time (but not too much) working up a song which he seems to have regarded from the start as a blatant piece of filler.

REVOLUTION 9
JOHN LENNON/PAUL McCARTNEY
RECORDED 30, 31 MAY 4, 6, 10, 11, 20, 21, JUNE
16 SEPTEMBER 1968

On the raucous collage of sounds that was the second half of the original 'Revolution 1' (see above), John Lennon and Yoko Ono built an aural nightmare, intended to capture the atmosphere of a violent revolution in progress. By far the most time-consuming 'White Album' track to complete, and then the most controversial when the record was released, 'Revolution 9' was John and Yoko's most successful venture into the world of sound-as-art.

The track began bizarrely enough, with a snippet of an unreleased Paul McCartney song (see 'I Will'), then an EMI test tape repeating the words "Number nine" over and over again. After that, there was chaos – a cavalcade of tape loops, feedback, impromptu screams and carefully rehearsed vocal overdubs, sound effects recordings and the noise of a society disintegrating. Reportedly, Paul McCartney agreed to the inclusion of the track only with severe misgivings, which George Martin expressed more forcibly.

GOOD NIGHT
JOHN LENNON/PAUL McCARTNEY
RECORDED 28 JUNE, 2, 22 JULY 1968

The composer of this lush and sentimental ballad was not the lush and sentimental Paul McCartney, but the acerbic and cynical John Lennon, whose contributions to 'The White Album' therefore ranged from the ultra-weird to the ultra-romantic within two consecutive tracks. Fast becoming the children's favourite of The Beatles, Ringo Starr sang this lullaby, to a purely orchestral accompaniment. None of the other three Beatles appears on the track.

Yellow Submarine

PARLOPHONE

CDP7 46445 2

The decision to base a cartoon film on a fictionalised version of the 1967 Beatles, named after one of their best-loved songs and featuring characters loosely taken from several others, brought to an end a stand-off which had been threatening to become embarrassing. Ever since they'd completed Help! in the summer of 1965, The Beatles had owed United Artists another film. Initially, they'd swallowed their lack of enthusiasm for another comic romp, and considered various scripts submitted in late 1965 and early 1966. A year after that, Brian Epstein was still promising the outside world that the movie would shortly begin production – though no final script or concept was ever agreed.

One of Epstein's last important deals before his death was his agreement to assist with the making of a *Yellow Submarine*, which would require little or no active involvement from The Beatles, bar the submission of several new songs. The group did not even have to supply the voices for their cartoon selves, actors taking over the role, and creating a minor press 'scandal' in the process.

As it turned out, The Beatles were so delighted by the finished cartoon – having expected crassness and been shown something close to art – that they agreed to appear in a final real-life scene, giving their public approval to the movie.

Until then, however, their contribution had been minimal. Until the film company's schedule demanded final delivery of the songs, they'd mentally set aside any rejects from 1967 sessions for the movie. The balance of power in the group dictated that two of the four rejects were George Harrison compositions – one of them the most striking piece of psychedelia The Beatles ever recorded.

These four new songs were originally planned for release as an EP. This was considered unsuitable for the American market, however, and so an album was concocted, combining the new items with two old songs from the soundtrack, plus twenty minutes of George Martin's incidental music. The group presumably decided against an LP made up of all their film songs because it would have repeated too many of the numbers from the 'Sgt. Pepper' and 'Magical Mystery Tour' albums.

YELLOW SUBMARINE
JOHN LENNON/PAUL McCARTNEY
RECORDED 26 MAY, 1 JUNE 1966

Unchanged from its appearance on 'Revolver', the title song from the *Yellow Submarine* cartoon was one of two songs making its second appearance on a Beatles record.

ONLY A NORTHERN SONG
GEORGE HARRISON
RECORDED 13, 14 FEBRUARY, 20 APRIL 1967

"A joke relating to Liverpool, the Holy City in the North of England," is how George Harrison described this song – bizarrely never issued in 'true' stereo. The joke, incidentally, refers to Northern Songs, the company who published compositions by Lennon, McCartney and (in 1967, at least) Harrison. The lyrical *non sequiturs* and lugubrious

musical backing made this one of the more unusual Beatles recordings, even by 1967 standards.

ALL TOGETHER NOW
JOHN LENNON/PAUL McCARTNEY
RECORDED 12 MAY 1967

Written with the film very much in mind, McCartney's singalong ditty became a children's favourite, completed in just over five hours of studio work. It's hard to imagine a song this slight being considered for any of the other Beatles albums.

HEY BULLDOG
JOHN LENNON/PAUL McCARTNEY
RECORDED 11 FEBRUARY 1968

"I went to see The Beatles recording, and I said to John, 'Why do you always use that beat all the time, the same beat, why don't you do something more complex?'" Yoko Ono's question mightn't have been the most tactful way of greeting her first sight of her husband-to-be at work. On this occasion, in fact, simplicity was bliss. Gathered in the studio to shoot a promo film for the 'Lady Madonna' single, The Beatles made use of the opportunity to complete their obligations to the film company. Like 'I Am The Walrus', 'Hey Bulldog' defied detailed lyrical analysis, but its wonderfully chaotic production and raw Lennon vocal made it a minor classic. The Beatles enjoyed it, too, as a listen to the fade-out makes clear.

IT'S ALL TOO MUCH
GEORGE HARRISON
RECORDED 25, 26 MAY, 2 JUNE 1967

This song, said composer George Harrison, was "written in a childlike manner from realisations that appeared during and after some LSD experiences and which were later confirmed in meditation." It was also a wonderfully inventive piece of psychedelia, a spirit-of-'67 freak-out that won fresh acclaim from a later wave of acid-rock adventurers in the late Seventies and early Nineties. Discordant, offbeat and effortlessly brilliant, the song was (alongside 'Taxman') Harrison's finest piece of Western rock music to date. Sadly, it was edited before release, losing one verse in its reduction from eight minutes to six.

ALL YOU NEED IS LOVE
JOHN LENNON/PAUL McCARTNEY
RECORDED 14, 19, 23, 24, 25 JUNE 1967

Fanatics please note: the mix of this song included on the 'Yellow Submarine' album was marginally different from the original hit single.

Remaining tracks by George Martin

PEPPERLAND
SEA OF TIME & SEA OF HOLES
SEA OF MONSTERS
MARCH OF THE MEANIES
PEPPERLAND LAID WASTE
GEORGE MARTIN

YELLOW SUBMARINE IN PEPPERLAND
JOHN LENNON/PAUL McCARTNEY
ARRANGED BY GEORGE MARTIN

Aside from Martin's orchestral revamp of the film's title song, these attractive instrumental numbers had no connection with The Beatles. Their presence on the CD makes 'Yellow Submarine' the least inspiring of The Beatles' albums for all but the determined completist.

Abbey Road

PARLOPHONE
CDP7 46446 2

The Beatles finished work on 'The White Album' in October 1968. It was released in November, followed in January 1969 by the Yellow Submarine soundtrack LP. That month, The Beatles also recorded what eventually became the 'Let It Be' LP. And three weeks after the end of the basic sessions for that record, the group began work on another new album. Within the space of a year, then, The Beatles recorded or released around 60 new songs. So you'd expect the last of these albums to suffer in the songwriting stakes. 'Abbey Road' may have its throwaways, especially in the lengthy medley on the original second side of the LP, but many fans regard it as the best album The Beatles ever made. It's also their best selling album.

That isn't a view that John Lennon would have backed, though. He regarded the album as contrived, a deliberate repair-job on The Beatles' image after the disastrous 'Let It Be' sessions. Producer George Martin had a more balanced view of 'Abbey Road': "That whole album was a compromise. One side was a whole series of titles which John preferred and the other side was a programme Paul and I preferred. I had been trying to get them to think in symphonic terms and think of the entire shape of the album and getting some form to it – symphonic things like bringing songs back in counterpoint to other songs, actually shaped things. And I think if we had gone on making records, that was the way I would have done it. But we were already breaking up. 'Abbey Road' was the death knell."

Martin's admission that he sided with Paul's concept for the record rather than John's is a tacit admission that the trio's working relationship had become irretrievably fragile.

Lennon's response was virtually to withdraw from the sessions. 'Abbey Road' is very much a McCartney album, with strong cameos from George Harrison: Lennon's material either sat uneasily alongside the rest of the songs, or else was little more than hackwork.

And yet: The Beatles never played or sang together more brilliantly than they did on 'Abbey Road'. In particular, the much-maligned Side Two medley – assembled from a collection of vignettes – is instrumentally tighter than anything they'd cut since 'Revolver'. And never had The Beatles' harmony vocals been more inventive, or stunningly precise, than on this record. Countless times on the album there are moments of pure beauty, proof that art can sometimes force its way to the surface almost against the wishes of its creators.

COME TOGETHER
JOHN LENNON/PAUL McCARTNEY
RECORDED 21, 22, 23, 25, 29, 30 JULY 1969

During the Lennons' Toronto bed-in in May 1969, one visitor to their humble hotel room was Timothy Leary, LSD guru and would-be liberator of the world's collective mind. Leary had decided to run for Congress, or the Senate, or anywhere that would have him, and had decided on a campaign slogan: 'Come together'. Knowing Lennon to have been a keen user of his favourite drug, Leary commissioned John to write a song of that title, which his followers could sing on the campaign trail.

Lennon did as he was asked, and came up with a banal ditty along the lines of "Come together and join the party". Then Leary went to jail. Lennon reckoned his obligations had now expired, and used the "come together" idea for himself. Instead of a political anthem, 'Come Together' became a celebration of marital sex, with verses that free-associated Chuck Berry style. (In fact, Lennon borrowed a little too blatantly from Berry's 'You Can't Catch Me', sparking a legal dispute that was still affecting his career six years later.)

In the studio, Lennon prefaced the song with a whispered refrain of "shoot" – which gained an unwelcome dose of irony 11 years later. The Beatles' version never quite caught fire, however, and Lennon remained fonder of the live remake he taped in 1972 at Madison Square Garden.

SOMETHING
GEORGE HARRISON
RECORDED 2, 5 MAY, 11, 16 JULY, 15 AUGUST 1969

What Frank Sinatra called "the greatest love song ever written", and he'd sung a few in his time, began life in 1968, when George Harrison listened to a track on one of the first batch of Apple Records LPs. The track in question was James Taylor's 'Something In The Way She Moves', and Harrison soon built a song around the phrase – little realising that it would become his best-known and most lucrative composition.

After recording a solo demo of 'Something' in February 1969, Harrison brought it to the 'Abbey Road' sessions in April. An initial attempt to cut the backing track was rejected; so the band, plus Billy Preston, regrouped early in May. At that point, the track lasted nearly eight minutes, ending in a rather low-key instrumental jam which was subsequently edited out of the mix. Sporadically over the next two months, Harrison added to the basic track, the final session featuring overdubs from 21 string players.

As he did later with 'My Sweet Lord' and 'All Things Must Pass', George had already given one of his best songs away to a friend by the time he recorded it himself. The recipient this time was Joe Cocker, though luckily for The Beatles his version appeared only after theirs. The Beatles' rendition, meanwhile, went on to become the first UK single pulled from one of their previously released albums, plus Harrison's first Beatles A-side.

The song reached a wider currency via Sinatra's regular performances. Tailoring the lyric to his own needs, Ol' Blue Eyes rewrote part of the middle section: "You stick around, Jack, she might show". Amused by this bastardisation of his work, George retained Sinatra's phrasing when he performed the song live in the early 90s.

MAXWELL'S SILVER HAMMER
JOHN LENNON/PAUL McCARTNEY
RECORDED 9, 10, 11 JULY, 6 AUGUST 1969

To judge from the general level of enthusiasm on display when the song is performed in the *Let It Be* movie, no-one had much time for 'Maxwell's Silver Hammer' apart from its composer, Paul McCartney. A novelty song about a serial killer, it was distinguished by its blatant commercial appeal, and for its subtle use of a prototype Moog synthesiser by Paul.

OH! DARLING
JOHN LENNON/PAUL McCARTNEY
RECORDED 20, 26 APRIL, 17, 18, 22, 23 JULY, 8, 11 AUGUST 1969

To his dying day, John Lennon resented the fact that Paul McCartney didn't ask him to sing the throat-shredding lead vocal on this 50s-styled rocker. At session after session, in fact, McCartney would arrive early to attempt a take before his voice lost its flexibility. Eventually he nailed it, completing a performance that later inspired a 'tribute' of sorts, in the shape of 10cc's 'Oh Donna'.

OCTOPUS'S GARDEN
RICHARD STARKEY
RECORDED 26, 29 APRIL, 17, 18 JULY 1969

As seen in the *Let It Be* movie, Ringo Starr arrived at the Apple Studios one day with the idea for a song. George Harrison turned it into one, rewriting the chord sequence, and suggesting ways in which the melody could be improved. With no egos at stake when a Ringo song was on the menu, The Beatles lent themselves whole-heartedly to the playful spirit of the song. Ringo revived memories of 'Yellow Submarine' with some suitably aquatic sound effects.

I WANT YOU (SHE'S SO HEAVY)
JOHN LENNON/PAUL McCARTNEY
RECORDED 22, 23 FEBRUARY, 18, 20 APRIL, 8, 11, 20 AUGUST 1969

The first of the 'Abbey Road' songs to be started was one of the last to be finished – and also the only Lennon composition on the album that sounded as if it came from the heart. Deliberately unpoetic, it was a simple cry of love for Yoko Ono, with a bluesy verse (based around the rhythm of the mid-Sixties Mel Torme hit, 'Coming Home Baby') locked to a relentless, multi-overdub guitar riff, concocted by Lennon and Harrison.

Besides the relentless plod of the guitar battalions, the closing minutes of the track resounded to the hiss and moan of the Moog

synthesiser, adding an unearthly menace to what began as a simple song of love and lust.

HERE COMES THE SUN
GEORGE HARRISON

RECORDED 7, 8, 16 JULY, 6, 11, 15, 19 AUGUST 1969

Faced with a day of business meetings at Apple, George Harrison repaired to Eric Clapton's garden, where he wrote this beautiful song around some simple variations on a D-chord. Another instant classic to set alongside 'Something', it revealed Harrison as the dark horse of the group, rapidly rivalling his more prestigious bandmates. Once again, some delicate Moog touches enhanced the final mix.

BECAUSE
JOHN LENNON/PAUL McCARTNEY

RECORDED 1, 4, 5 AUGUST 1969

Though John Lennon later nailed this track as "a terrible arrangement", most fans regard it as one of the highlights of 'Abbey Road' – both for the beauty of its lyrics (a pantheistic vision that was closer to romantic poetry than

acid-inspired fantasy) and for the stunning three-part harmonies of Harrison, Lennon and McCartney. Lennon wrote the song around a piano riff he found when he asked Yoko to play Beethoven's 'Moonlight Sonata' – backwards.

YOU NEVER GIVE ME YOUR MONEY
JOHN LENNON/PAUL McCARTNEY

RECORDED 6 MAY, 1, 11, 15, 30, 31 JULY, 5 AUGUST 1969

"'Abbey Road' was really unfinished songs all stuck together," complained John Lennon in 1980. "Everybody praises the album so much, but none of the songs had anything to do with each other, no thread at all, only the fact that we stuck them together."

That's true, but it ignores the fact that the medley – which began with this song, and climaxed some fifteen minutes later with 'The End' – was great pop music, with a cascade of hooks, mini-choruses and themes interlocking to produce a tapestry of melody and sound.

'You Never Give Me Your Money' is the strongest of the medley songs. It began life as an ironic comment on The Beatles' business disputes, and achieved the same oblique lyrical significance as McCartney's best songs on 'Pepper'. Within four minutes, it moves through five distinct sections without once appearing contrived.

SUN KING
JOHN LENNON/PAUL McCARTNEY
RECORDED 24, 25, 29 JULY 1969

'Sun King' revamped the guitar picking technique Lennon had used on 'Julia' the previous year, matched with the vocal harmonies of 'Because'. The song was a complete throwaway – most of the lyrics were mock-Spanish gobbledegook – but it *sounded* wonderful.

MEAN MR. MUSTARD
JOHN LENNON/PAUL McCARTNEY
RECORDED 24, 25, 29 JULY 1969

Originally up for consideration for 'The White Album', 'Mean Mr Mustard' was a Lennon fantasy which he'd based around a newspaper story about a notorious miser. Though it has an entirely different feel to 'Sun King', the two songs were recorded together as one musical piece, under the working title of 'Here Comes The Sun-King'.

POLYTHENE PAM
JOHN LENNON/PAUL McCARTNEY
RECORDED 25, 28 JULY 1969

Demonstrating that the medley was planned from the start, 'Polythene Pam' and 'She Came In Through The Bathroom Window' were also recorded as one. 'Polythene Pam', showing off John Lennon's best Scouser accent, was based loosely around a character he'd met in a near-orgy the previous year. It led seamlessly into...

SHE CAME IN THROUGH THE BATHROOM WINDOW
JOHN LENNON/PAUL McCARTNEY
RECORDED 25, 28 JULY 1969

Like its companion piece, 'She Came In Through The Bathroom Window' was loosely autobiographical – the spur this time being an attempted robbery at Paul McCartney's house, in which a fan had climbed in through aforesaid window in search of first-hand

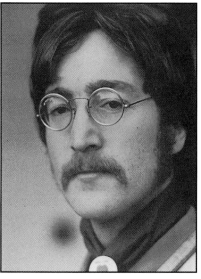

GOLDEN SLUMBERS
JOHN LENNON/PAUL McCARTNEY
RECORDED 2, 3, 4, 30, 31 JULY, 15 AUGUST 1969

Thomas Dekker's 17th century lullaby took musical shape in Paul McCartney's hand, with one of those melodies that was entirely original but sounded on first hearing as if you'd known it your entire life. Once again, the song was recorded from the start as part of a medley with...

CARRY THAT WEIGHT
JOHN LENNON/PAUL McCARTNEY
RECORDED 2, 3, 4, 30, 31 JULY, 15 AUGUST 1969

Another McCartney composition, this reprised some of the lyrical and musical themes of 'You Never Give Me Your Money', and featured mass vocals from McCartney, Harrison and Starr. Lennon missed the sessions for this song, being otherwise detained in a Scottish hospital after a car crash.

souvenirs. And like 'Something', a cover of this song ended up on Joe Cocker's second album, part of The Beatles' thank-you for Cocker's remarkable interpretation of 'With A Little Help From My Friends'.

THE END
JOHN LENNON/PAUL McCARTNEY
RECORDED 23 JULY, 5, 7, 8, 15, 18 AUGUST 1969

'Carry That Weight' sounds as if it had been taped at the same time as 'The End', but the latter was actually inserted over the fade-out of 'Carry That Weight' as an entirely separate recording. It features two lines of vocals, the second of which became something of a valediction to The Beatles: "And in the end, the love you make is equal to the love you take". There was Ringo's one and only drum solo on record, and a lengthy guitar section which featured interplay between Harrison, Lennon and McCartney. An orchestra was added to the final seconds of the song – all part of the extravaganza which provided a fitting finale to The Beatles' longest and most carefully structured suite of songs.

HER MAJESTY
JOHN LENNON/PAUL McCARTNEY
RECORDED 2 JULY 1969

It wasn't quite 'The End', though. At the close of a tape carrying a rough mix of the second side of the album, engineer John Kurlander inserted a brief 20-second ditty which had originally been meant to appear between 'Mean Mr Mustard' and 'Polythene Pam', until Paul McCartney decided he wanted it removed. When another engineer, Malcolm Davies, cut an acetate of the side, he assumed 'Her Majesty' was meant to be the final track. Paul liked the surprise element of including the song on the album – even though it began with the final chord of 'Mean Mr Mustard', while its own final chord was missing, hidden beneath the opening flurry of 'Polythene Pam'. Just as the chaos of 'You Know My Name (Look Up The Number)' brought The Beatles' singles career to a tongue-in-cheek close, 'Her Majesty' prevented anyone from claiming that the group's lengthy 'Abbey Road' medley was a sign of pomposity.

LET IT BE

Let It Be

PARLOPHONE

CDP7 46447 2

In November 1968, Paul McCartney finally realised that The Beatles were on the verge of internal collapse. Faced with the alternative of letting the group slip away, or fighting for their future, he made a decisive move. John Lennon and George Harrison had made their opposition to performing live with The Beatles very clear; Ringo Starr, meanwhile, was happy to go with the flow. But for one last time, McCartney persuaded the group to think again – to regain contact with their core audience by performing one, or at most two, live concerts, which would be filmed for a TV special. Maybe there'd be two TV shows in the deal, one covering the rehearsals, the other the concert. And the live performance would in turn become The Beatles' next album – a deliberate opposite to the months-long sessions for 'Sgt. Pepper' and 'The Beatles'.

Dates were booked at the Albert Hall, then the Roundhouse, for December; but the plans fell through. Harrison's opposition proved to be the crucial factor, but he did agree to film cameras documenting the band at work, with the possibility of a live show if the rehearsals went well enough.

So on January 2nd 1969, The Beatles assembled at Twickenham Film Studios for the first of three weeks' of fraught 'private' rehearsals. "It was a dreadful feeling in Twickenham Studios being filmed all the time," said John Lennon after the trauma was over. "I just wanted them to go away. We'd be there at eight in the morning and you couldn't make music at that time. It was in a strange place with people filming and coloured lights."

Towards the end of the month, the venue moved to the group's own, newly-opened Apple Studios, where they were joined by Beatle-for-a-fortnight Billy Preston, whose presence helped calm the group's internal friction. There they attempted to record a 'live-in-the-studio' LP, taping hour after hour of ramshackle recordings. On January 30, they played their concert – on the roof of the Apple building, a couple of hundred feet above any possible audience. The next day, they performed several more songs live in front of the cameras, within the safety of the Apple studios. Then they dumped the tapes on engineer Glyn Johns, and told him to go away and come up with an album. Three weeks into February, they had already begun work on 'Abbey Road'.

"We didn't want to know," Lennon admitted. "We just left it to Glyn and said, here, do it. It's the first time since the first album that we didn't have anything to do with it. None of us could be bothered going in. We were going to let it out with a really shitty condition, to show people what had happened to us."

Johns completed work on one version of the album, provisionally titled 'Get Back', in May; The Beatles rejected it. 'Abbey Road' concentrated their attention for a while; then John Lennon told the others he was quitting the group. In January 1970, the remaining three Beatles taped one more song, and a

final batch of overdubs, and Glyn Johns prepared a second 'Get Back' LP. It too was turned down by all the group.

Enter legendary American producer Phil Spector, who'd been touting for work with The Beatles. In March 1970, he began an intensive week of remixing and overdubbing. In the first week of May, the LP – retitled 'Let It Be', and packaged with a *Get Back* photo book that had been intended for the original album – was in the shops.

"When Spector came, it was 'go and do your audition'," Lennon explained. "And he worked like a pig on it. He'd always wanted to work with The Beatles and he was given the shittiest load of badly recorded shit with a lousy feeling to it ever, and he made something out of it. He did a great job. When I heard it, I didn't puke."

Paul McCartney did, though, appalled by the orchestral and choral overdubs added to his song, 'The Long And Winding Road'. Critics slated the album, and by the time the documentary film of the original sessions was released, McCartney had announced that he was leaving the group. Lennon's prior decision having been kept out of the media, he was promptly blamed for the break-up. By the end of 1970, Paul was suing the rest of the band in the High Court. As John Lennon put it, the dream was over.

TWO OF US
JOHN LENNON/PAUL McCARTNEY
RECORDED 31 JANUARY 1969

As the movie demonstrated, 'Two Of Us' began its life as a playful rocker, but quickly mutated into a gentle McCartney acoustic song – its title and duet format a final gesture of affection from Paul to John. The live-in-the-studio recording from January 1969 was brilliantly enhanced by Phil Spector's post-production, which gave the acoustic instruments a richness missing from any previous Beatles recording.

DIG A PONY
JOHN LENNON/PAUL McCARTNEY
RECORDED 30 JANUARY 1969

Edited down slightly from the rooftop recording, this was a typically obscure Lennon song, full of lines which promised much and never quite delivered. In the early years of the group, he'd concocted fictional love songs at will; in their closing months, he was equally capable of manufacturing lyrics that hinted at a spiritual depth they didn't possess. Understandably, Lennon was sniffy about the song in later years.

ACROSS THE UNIVERSE
JOHN LENNON/PAUL McCARTNEY
RECORDED 4, 8 FEBRUARY 1968, 1 APRIL 1970

John was anything but sniffy about 'Across The Universe', however. "It's one of the best lyrics I've written," he said proudly in 1970, "in fact it could be *the* best. It's good poetry, or whatever you call it. The ones I like are the ones that stand as words without melody." Composed in a stream-of-consciousness, early-hours lyrical torrent, it belongs in the category of poetry that describes its own creation, standing as a hymn of praise to whatever muse gave it birth. But Lennon never matched that sense of freedom in the recording studio. Originally taped in the same batch of sessions that produced 'Lady Madonna', the song was left to one side while the group decided what to do with it. First it was going to be a single, then a flipside, then an EP cut. It was revived unsuccessfully during the film sessions, but without a hint of inspiration. Finally, it was given away to the World Wildlife Fund for a charity album.

Phil Spector took the original tape, slowed it down a fraction, deleted the overdubbed bird sounds (see 'PAST MASTERS 2'), and added an orchestra and a choir. The result was one of the highlights of The Beatles' career, justification in itself for Spector's involvement in the creative process.

I ME MINE
GEORGE HARRISON
RECORDED 3 JANUARY, 1, 2 APRIL 1970

For the last time, The Beatles gathered together in one place early in January 1970. Only one thing was wrong: The Beatles were now a three-piece, without John Lennon, who was having his hair cut and discovering the secret of how flying saucers worked in Denmark.

Cutting Harrison's tune – half waltz, half rocker – without Lennon wasn't a problem: the three other Beatles had performed it that way in the *Let It Be* movie, while John and Yoko danced around the studio floor.

McCartney, Harrison and Starr ended up with a song barely 90 seconds long: Phil Spector simply copied chunks of the tape and nearly doubled its length.

DIG IT
JOHN LENNON/PAUL McCARTNEY/GEORGE HARRISON/RICHARD STARKEY
RECORDED 26 JANUARY 1969

A brief extract from an improvised three-chord jam session that ran to more than 12 minutes on tape, 'Dig It' was included on the album to boost its verité credentials. The original 'Get Back' LP would have included a longer chunk of the song, to no-one's great benefit. Check the hours of session tapes that have emerged from movie off-cuts, and you'll find that The Beatles were infatuated by the phrase 'dig it' in January 1969. They could have assembled a full album of their jams around the phrase, but thankfully resisted the temptation.

LET IT BE
JOHN LENNON/PAUL McCARTNEY
RECORDED 31 JANUARY, 30 APRIL 1969, 4 JANUARY 1970

The Beatles' final single, and by far the strongest song débuted during the sessions, 'Let It Be' was a rare piece of spiritually-inspired writing from Paul McCartney. The 'Mother Mary' in the lyric was universally assumed to be his own mother, the late Mary McCartney, while the conciliatory tone of the song might have been an overt message of peace to the other Beatles.

Originally taped in front of the cameras in January 1969, the song was overdubbed with a lead guitar solo in April; then again with another in January 1970, at the same session in which a George Martin-scored brass section was overdubbed.

The first guitar solo appeared on the single; for this album mix, Phil Spector selected the rawer second effort, and also heightened the sound of Ringo and Paul's percussion, to the point where it threatened to become intrusive.

MAGGIE MAE
Trad. arr. JOHN LENNON/PAUL McCARTNEY
GEORGE HARRISON/RICHARD STARKEY
RECORDED 24 JANUARY 1969

Recorded between takes of 'Two Of Us', this was a 30-second, Lennon-led revival of a popular Liverpool folksong – rescued from the session tapes by George Martin and producer/engineer Glyn Johns.

I'VE GOT A FEELING
JOHN LENNON/PAUL McCARTNEY
RECORDED 30 JANUARY 1969

Mix an unfinished McCartney blues called 'I've Got A Feeling' with an unfinished Lennon acoustic ballad called 'Everybody Had A Hard Year', and you had one of the roughest and most impressive songs on the 'Let It Be' album – taped during the Apple rooftop concert. This was the last song that Lennon and McCartney actively wrote as a songwriting partnership.

ONE AFTER 909
JOHN LENNON/PAUL McCARTNEY
RECORDED 30 JANUARY 1969

'One After 909' joined 'What Goes On', 'When I'm Sixty-Four' and 'I'll Follow The Sun' on the list of pre-1960 Beatles songs released on official albums. Originally composed by John Lennon as an American-style rocker in 1959, the song was revived as a possible single in March 1963, though that version remains unreleased. Six years later, something reminded Lennon of the song, and he re-introduced it to the group's repertoire in time for the *Let It Be* film, and the rooftop concert at Apple in particular. Maybe not coincidentally, The Beatles sounded more relaxed playing this oldie in semi-satirical style than anywhere else in the movie.

THE LONG AND WINDING ROAD
JOHN LENNON/PAUL McCARTNEY
RECORDED 31 JANUARY 1969, 1 APRIL 1970

One of the two great McCartney ballads premièred during these ill-fated sessions, 'The Long And Winding Road' began life as a gentle, piano-based performance, with mild accompaniment from the rest of The Beatles. In the hands of producer Phil Spector, however, it became a production extravaganza, with 50 musicians and vocalists overdubbed onto the basic track. McCartney hated the results, complaining that Spector had swamped his work with a Mantovani-style arrangement; Spector's defenders said that Phil had simply responded to the natural romanticism of the song. Paul also moaned about the presence of female vocalists on the track, which was somewhat ironic in view of his subsequent recording career.

FOR YOU BLUE
GEORGE HARRISON
RECORDED 25 JANUARY 1969

Harrison's slide-guitar blues – with John 'Elmore' Lennon on slide – was a slight but appealing song that fitted in well with the album's original, live-in-the-studio concept. It was one of the few tracks on the album taken from the early days of recording at Apple, rather than the rooftop concert or the subsequent 'before-the-cameras' session.

GET BACK
JOHN LENNON/PAUL McCARTNEY
RECORDED 27 JANUARY 1969

'Get Back' ended the *Let It Be* film, and the album, in 1970; and the same charming piece of Lennon dialogue ("I hope we passed the audition") followed it on both occasions. But the two versions of 'Get Back' were entirely different, the rooftop performance appearing in the film, while the LP ended with an Apple studios take that was recorded three days earlier. A longer version of the song had already been issued as a single in April 1969 (see 'PAST MASTERS 2').

THE BEATLES

PAST MASTERS · VOLUME ONE

Past Masters Volume I

PARLOPHONE

CDP7 90043 2

Once EMI had issued all the original UK Beatles albums on CD, they were left with several options for completing the digital transfer of the entire back catalogue. Happily, they chose the most sensible, collecting together all the leftover tracks, in (more or less) chronological order, across two CDs. Included were their non-LP singles (including the different versions of 'Love Me Do', 'Get Back' and 'Let It Be' from those on LPs), the songs from the 'Long Tall Sally' EP, the two German-language tracks from 1964, the elusive 'Bad Boy' from 1965, and the 'original' mix of 'Across The Universe', only previously issued on a budget charity LP. EMI resisted the temptation to flesh out the packages with 'rarities' like mono mixes and marginally different edits that had appeared in Britain and around the world, though the specialist market would no doubt relish a CD or two of these minor delights.

LOVE ME DO

JOHN LENNON/PAUL McCARTNEY

RECORDED 4 SEPTEMBER 1962

"Our greatest philosophical song," Paul McCartney called it tongue-in-cheek. But it was, in this original version with Ringo Starr on drums, The Beatles' first single, later replaced on album and 45 by the version available on the 'Please Please Me' CD.

FROM ME TO YOU

JOHN LENNON/PAUL McCARTNEY

RECORDED 5 MARCH 1963

On the bus between York and Shrewsbury, on 28 February 1963, John Lennon and Paul McCartney wrote the third Beatles' single. Like many of their early songs, it was deliberately built around heavy use of personal pronouns – the idea being that their audience could easily identify with the 'me' and 'you' in the title.

The opening harmonica solo was George Martin's suggestion, and proved to be a major part of the record's appeal. Equally commercial was the simple melody line of the chorus, which leaves 'From Me To You' as one of the less durable Beatles 45s.

THANK YOU GIRL
JOHN LENNON/PAUL McCARTNEY
RECORDED 5, 13 MARCH 1963

Songwriting for The Beatles in 1963 was less about self-expression than it was about a constant search for hit records. John Lennon's 'Thank You Girl' was one of the attempts that didn't quite make it, despite all the usual ingredients – his harmonica showcase, an easy-on-the-ear melody and a vocal gimmick. This time simplicity was taken a step too far, and 'Thank You Girl' wouldn't have withstood the constant airplay that every Beatles single was treated to in the Sixties.

SHE LOVES YOU
JOHN LENNON/PAUL McCARTNEY
RECORDED 1 JULY 1963

"People said at the time that this was the worst song we'd ever thought of doing," Paul McCartney mused in 1980, and the reviews of their fourth single were a trifle sniffy, suggesting that the group were struggling for new material. Instead, 'She Loves You' proved to be the anthem of Beatlemania. It's not the strongest song they recorded in 1963, or perhaps the most important (that honour must go to 'I Want To Hold Your Hand', which broke them in America), but more than anything else, it conjures up the exuberance which so entranced the nation in the latter half of 1963.

George Martin regarded the final vocal harmony as a cliché, which it may have been in classical terms, but to the pop audience it was a revelation. What sold the record, and The Beatles, though, was the sheer inane appeal of the chorus. Even now, repeat the phrase 'yeah, yeah, yeah' to almost anyone in the country, and they'll catch the reference to The Beatles.

I'LL GET YOU

JOHN LENNON/PAUL McCARTNEY

RECORDED 1 JULY 1963

Like 'Thank You Girl' this Lennon number came straight off the production line, though this time the melody line wasn't quite catchy enough for a single. Take note of the middle eight, however, where John demonstrated that he was every bit as strong a tunesmith as McCartney.

I WANT TO HOLD YOUR HAND

JOHN LENNON/PAUL McCARTNEY

RECORDED 17 OCTOBER 1963

"We wrote that together," John admitted after The Beatles split up, in a rare nod of the head to his ex-partner. "It's a beautiful melody – the kind of song I like to sing." And it broke The Beatles as a worldwide phenomenon, becoming their first No. 1 in America, and indeed topping the charts in almost every part of the globe. Cunningly structured, with a drop in tension in the middle section leading to the climactic "I can't hide" (memorably misheard by Bob Dylan as "I get high"), the song was the culmination of a solid year of experimentation and learning by The Beatles' creative axis.

THIS BOY

JOHN LENNON/PAUL McCARTNEY

RECORDED 17 OCTOBER 1963

The first great three-part harmony vehicle in The Beatles catalogue was written by John Lennon around the standard doo-wop chord changes that had fuelled hundreds of hit records in the 50s. What made the song was not just the tightness of the harmonies, but the sheer liberation of the middle section – Lennon stretching out the final syllable over several bars. The Beatles accentuated the drama of the moment less on record than they did subsequently on stage, where it rivalled the two-heads-shaking-at-one-microphone routine for audience response. 'This Boy' made an ideal underbelly for the 'I Want To Hold Your Hand' single.

KOMM, GIB MIR DEINE HAND

JOHN LENNON/PAUL McCARTNEY
NICOLAS/HELLMER

RECORDED 29 JANUARY 1964

It was in Paris, bizarrely enough, that The Beatles recorded German-language renditions of their two most recent singles. Most recording stars of the time were required to re-cut their hits in European languages, but having endured the process once, The Beatles said never again. This translation of 'I Want To Hold Your Hand' was marginally the more successful of the two tracks, using the original backing plus overdubbed handclapping.

SIE LIEBT DICH

JOHN LENNON/PAUL McCARTNEY
NICOLAS/MONTAGUE

RECORDED 29 JANUARY 1964

The original tape of the English 'She Loves You' had already been destroyed when this German version was required, so The Beatles had to re-record the song from the top, skipping through it with only minor attention to detail.

LONG TALL SALLY

RICHARD PENNIMAN/ENOTRIS JOHNSON/ROBERT BLACKWELL

RECORDED 1 MARCH 1964

In just one magnificent take, with no overdubs, The Beatles recorded the finest rock'n'roll performance of their career – seizing Little Richard's 1956 classic and remaking it as their own. George Harrison's solo was spot-on first time, and George Martin duplicated Richard's piano-thumping. What clinched the track, though, was Paul McCartney's throat-searing lead vocal, his finest uptempo performance ever in a recording studio. The song became the title track of (appropriately enough) the group's best-ever EP.

I CALL YOUR NAME

JOHN LENNON/PAUL McCARTNEY

RECORDED 1 MARCH 1964

Already recorded by fellow Brian Epstein protégé Billy J. Kramer the previous year, this Lennon song was forcibly reclaimed by its composer on the 'Long Tall Sally' EP. John's dogmatic vocals suggested he didn't care whether the girl in question answered his call

or not, in stark contrast to Kramer's more submissive delivery. As Lennon remarked in 1980, the group approached the guitar solo as a ska band, loping slightly uncomfortably through the Jamaican rhythm before returning to more solid ground for the next verse.

SLOW DOWN
LARRY WILLIAMS
RECORDED 1, 4 JUNE 1964

Though it didn't quite match the sheer excitement of 'Long Tall Sally', Lennon's ultra-confident handling of the Larry Williams rocker (the first of three the band recorded) ran it close.

Aided by George Martin's piano, The Beatles cruised through this 12-bar, though it was the rasp in Lennon's voice that pushed it beyond the reach of their British beat group rivals.

MATCHBOX
CARL PERKINS
RECORDED 1 JUNE 1964

The Carl Perkins songbook was raided for the first time on the final 'Long Tall Sally' EP number. Ringo Starr was showcased on this rockabilly tune, based on lyrical ideas that had been circulating in the blues world for decades. The song's composer was on hand to witness the recording, which (alongside the two Perkins covers on 'Beatles For Sale') kept him in royalties for decades to come.

I FEEL FINE
JOHN LENNON/PAUL McCARTNEY
RECORDED 18 OCTOBER 1964

From the opening buzz of feedback (not a studio accident, as claimed at the time, but a conscious decision to use this electronic howl) to the cool passion of John Lennon's vocal, the group's final single of 1964 oozed quality and control. Lennon based the finger-twisting guitar riff on Bobby Parker's R&B record, 'Watch Your Step', which had been covered by The John Barry Seven as early as 1961, and was well known among British blues fans. But the smooth power of the song was Lennon's own, and hinted at The Beatles' development of the original beat-group sound which would follow in 1965.

SHE'S A WOMAN
JOHN LENNON/PAUL McCARTNEY
RECORDED 8 OCTOBER 1964

For once on a Beatles record, Lennon sounded more sophisticated than McCartney when 'I Feel Fine' was supported by the raucous 'She's A Woman'. Little more than an R&B jam with words, the track was hastily and erratically recorded – the stabbing rhythm guitar drops out a couple of times midway through – but it triumphed on sheer willpower.

BAD BOY
LARRY WILLIAMS
RECORDED 10 MAY 1965

On the same day that The Beatles recorded 'Dizzy Miss Lizzy', they also cut a more obscure Larry Williams rocker, 'Bad Boy'. Once again, John Lennon was to the fore, whooping his way through the tale of a pre-juvenile delinquent (told in true American slang). The group's instrumental support wasn't quite in the same league, which is probably why this track was reserved initially for an American LP, 'Beatles VI', and only appeared in Britain on the compilation, 'A Collection Of Beatles Oldies', in December 1966.

YES IT IS
JOHN LENNON/PAUL McCARTNEY
RECORDED 16 FEBRUARY 1965

George Harrison made the most of his first tone-pedal (alias 'wah-wah') in February 1965, using it on every possible song he could. It was one of several striking factors to this 1965 B-side, a successor to 'This Boy' as a vehicle for three-part harmony. In retrospect, it might have been better if they'd junked this initial attempt at the song and spent the time on rehearsals instead, as the beauty of the melody is rather undercut by the flat vocals on several lines.

I'M DOWN
JOHN LENNON/PAUL McCARTNEY
RECORDED 14 JUNE 1965

On the same day that McCartney recorded the folk-rocker 'I've Just Seen A Face' and the gentle ballad 'Yesterday', he also cut this raucous rock'n'roll song – the flipside of 'Help!' and a blatant attempt to write his own 'Long Tall Sally'. Indeed, 'I'm Down' replaced 'Long Tall Sally' as The Beatles' final song at almost every show they played in their last year as a live band. Despite having all the required ingredients, from Paul's raw vocal to George's stinging guitar solo, it never quite gelled as well as the Little Richard blueprint, and the lyrics seem rather misogynistic from the standpoint of the 1990s. But it's a powerful piece of work nonetheless.

THE BEATLES

PAST MASTERS · VOLUME TWO

Past Masters Volume II

PARLOPHONE

CDP7 90044 2

DAY TRIPPER

JOHN LENNON/PAUL McCARTNEY

RECORDED 16 OCTOBER 1965

For once, the guiding rule that you can tell which Beatle wrote a song by the identity of the lead vocalist breaks down with this song, originally issued as a double A-sided single in December 1965. 'Day Tripper' was a Lennon composition – the title apparently meant "a weekend hippie" – but it was McCartney who sang the verses, while Lennon handled the chorus. Like 'I Feel Fine' and 'Ticket To Ride', the song was built around a rock-solid guitar riff, which suggested that Lennon was responding to the inspiration of The Rolling Stones, who'd strung a series of singles around similar instrumental hook-lines since the middle of 1964.

WE CAN WORK IT OUT

JOHN LENNON/PAUL McCARTNEY

RECORDED 20, 29 OCTOBER 1965

Supporting 'Day Tripper' was this collaboration of two unfinished songs, taken by The Beatles themselves as revealing the diverse approaches of Lennon and McCartney to music and to life. EMI immediately tried to push this as the A-side of the single, only for John Lennon to intervene and insist that the rockier 'Day Tripper' be given equal, if not superior, status. Not that Lennon wanted to denigrate 'We Can Work It Out', to which he made a vital instrumental contribution on harmonium; he simply didn't wish to see the softer side of the group's music exposed at the expense of their rock'n'roll roots.

PAPERBACK WRITER
JOHN LENNON/PAUL McCARTNEY
RECORDED 13, 14 APRIL 1966

Widely greeted as a disappointment – a brash, insubstantial throwaway – at the time it was released, the first Beatles single of 1966 remains one of the jewels of The Beatles' crown, especially when coupled with its flipside, 'Rain'. It's true that Paul McCartney was writing a snapshot of fictional life rather than a confessional masterpiece or a straightforward teen romance, but the instrumental and vocal complexity of the song – plus its dazzling conceptual ambition – forced the ever-competitive Beach Boys to respond with the even more complex 'Good Vibrations'. The limits of EMI's studio technology were stretched to produce the richest, toughest sound of any Beatles record to date. Listen out for Lennon and Harrison's 'Frère Jacques' vocal refrain during the final verse, incidentally.

RAIN
JOHN LENNON/PAUL McCARTNEY
RECORDED 14, 16 APRIL 1966

Experimentation with drugs exploded John Lennon's creative potential. In place of the semi-fictional love songs that had been The Beatles' stock-in-trade, 1966 saw him introducing a series of numbers that explored the workings of the mind, and captured the hazy insight of the psychedelic experience.

'Rain' was one of the first, and perhaps the best, of his acid songs. Half dream, half nightmare in the wings, it combined the earthy, rich rock sound of its companion-piece, 'Paperback Writer', with an other-worldly lyric. The Beatles knew almost by instinct how to achieve that atmosphere in sound: they taped the backing track, complete with what Ringo regards as his best-ever drumming on record, at breakneck speed, then slowed the tape. Lennon's vocal went through the opposite process: it was recorded on a machine running slowly, and then speeded up for the final track. The juxtaposition of speed and laziness – plus the final burst of backwards vocals, an idea claimed by both Lennon and George Martin – heightened the unearthly tension of this brilliant record.

LADY MADONNA
JOHN LENNON/PAUL McCARTNEY
RECORDED 3, 6 FEBRUARY 1968

From its piano intro (lifted almost directly from Humphrey Lyttleton's mid-50s British jazz classic, 'Bad Penny Blues') to its rock'n'roll horn section, 'Lady Madonna' was the first Beatles single of 1968. It made a perfect introduction to a year when 50s rock'n'roll made a reappearance in the charts and the concert halls. The song itself was a more oblique piece of social comment than 'She's Leaving Home' the previous year, but its vague air of concern for a single mother fitted in with the contemporary trend for kitchen-sink drama in the theatre and on TV.

A bunch of Britain's top jazzmen were dragooned at short notice to play on the track, while Lennon, McCartney and Harrison faked one brass solo by blowing air through their cupped hands like children.

his final Indian-flavoured Beatles song, from the teachings of the Tao Te Ching, George put the matter straight in his autobiography. In that book, he printed a letter from Juan Mascaró, who translated the Tao, and actually sent George a copy of his translation of section XLVII, inviting him to set it to music.

Harrison duly did just that, composing perhaps the most beautiful melody of any of his 60s songs – which deserved a better fate than to languish on the flip of 'Lady Madonna'. The basic track for 'The Inner Light' was recorded at the same sessions as George's soundtrack music for the film *Wonderwall*, many thousands of miles away from Abbey Road – at EMI's studio in Bombay, India, to be exact. Various Indian musicians provided the instrumental backing. Several other raga-styled pieces were taped at the same session, but they remain unreleased.

THE INNER LIGHT
GEORGE HARRISON
RECORDED 12 JANUARY, 6, 8 FEBRUARY 1968

After several commentators had accused George Harrison of 'stealing' the lyrics to this,

HEY JUDE
JOHN LENNON/PAUL McCARTNEY
RECORDED 31 JULY, 1 AUGUST 1968

A couple of verses, a middle section or two, a fade-out: you can't explain the impact of 'Hey

Jude' by analysing the song. McCartney wrote the lyrics as a message of encouragement to young Julian Lennon, while his parents were in the throes of a very public separation. At times, the words veered into meaninglessness – "the movement you need is on your shoulder", indeed – and the tune was nothing complex. Neither was the production, which started simple and built towards an orchestral finale.

So why was 'Hey Jude' so important? Partly because of its length, though it was still shorter than another major 1968 hit, 'MacArthur Park' by Richard Harris. Mostly, though, 'Hey Jude' sounded like a community anthem, from the open-armed welcome of its lyrics to its instant singalong chorus. The fact that it didn't come with a controversial political message made its universal application complete.

At Trident Studios, The Beatles and a 36-piece orchestra recorded this remarkable record in two days – plus two beforehand for rehearsals. George Harrison's idea to answer McCartney's vocal lines with his electric guitar was vetoed, but John Lennon made his own distinctive contribution to the record with a

four-letter word, hidden deep in the mix around the three-minute mark.

REVOLUTION
JOHN LENNON/PAUL McCARTNEY
RECORDED 10, 11, 12 JULY 1968

'Revolution 1' (see 'THE BEATLES') was meant to be a single, but wasn't immediate enough. So John Lennon persuaded The Beatles to try again, setting his non-committal response to the worldwide uprisings of May 1968 to a fierce electric rhythm. With fuzzy, distorted guitars and a screaming vocal, 'Revolution' cut to the bone; it remains by far the toughest rock song The Beatles ever issued on a single. But Lennon's ambitions for the track weren't quite fulfilled, because the emergence of McCartney's 'Hey Jude' a month later made it quite clear what the lead track of The Beatles' first single on the Apple label would be. Still, John did have the compensation of knowing his song was on the flipside of the best-selling Beatles 45 of all time.

GET BACK
JOHN LENNON/PAUL McCARTNEY
RECORDED 28 JANUARY 1969

Shortly before his death, John Lennon revealed his long-felt suspicion that this song had been triggered by Paul McCartney's feelings towards Yoko. In fact, as he knew very well, 'Get Back' began life as an ironic comment on British politics. Under its original title of 'No Pakistanis', it satirised the racist views of those who saw Commonwealth immigrants as an invasion force, swamping British culture. Trouble was, the irony was likely to be lost on anyone who wasn't pre-warned, and McCartney regretfully dropped the original lyrics. (His decision was proved right nearly 20 years later when *The Sun* newspaper got hold of a tape of 'No Pakistanis', and accused The Beatles of racism. Irony is just too complicated for some people.)

In its new form, 'Get Back' was a tight, attractive rocker with lyrics that meant nothing but sounded good – a combination Paul tried to repeat, with rather less success, on Wings' singles like 'Helen Wheels' and 'Junior's Farm'. It featured a rare guitar showcase for John Lennon, who commented wryly: "When Paul was feeling kindly he would give me a solo, and I played the solo on that." Though 'Get Back' was performed on the Apple rooftop on 30 January 1969, the single version was taped in the studio a couple of days earlier, issued as a single in April (after emergency last-minute remixes) and then chopped down for inclusion on the 'Let It Be' LP in 1970.

DON'T LET ME DOWN
JOHN LENNON/PAUL McCARTNEY
RECORDED 28 JANUARY 1969

On the same day as 'Get Back', The Beatles recorded this gloriously spontaneous Lennon love song. For a brief moment, Lennon and McCartney were in perfect synchronisation, both of them keen to escape from the studio trickery and multi-overdubbing of recent Beatles albums. McCartney soon returned to over-production, on 'Abbey Road', but Lennon adopted the 'live-in-the-studio' approach as his watchword for the next couple of years.

THE BALLAD OF JOHN AND YOKO

JOHN LENNON/PAUL McCARTNEY

RECORDED 14 APRIL 1969

"Standing in the dock at Southampton/Trying to get to Holland or France..." Songs should be like newspapers, John Lennon said in 1970, and 'The Ballad Of John And Yoko' was just that – a report from the front-line in the battle between, on the one side, the keen-to-be-married Lennons, and on the other, the forces of law and order who didn't want convicted drugs offenders staging bed-ins in their capital cities, thank you very much.

'Instant' was John Lennon's approach to art in 1969 and 1970: his dream was to write a song in the morning, record it that afternoon, mix it at night and have it in the shops by the end of the week. He finally achieved that aim with his own 'Instant Karma!' early in 1970; but 'The Ballad Of John And Yoko' ran it close, being recorded and fully mixed in less than nine hours.

Such was the haste with which the session was arranged that only Paul McCartney was able to meet the call. He played drums to John's acoustic guitar for the basic track, and the two Beatles then overdubbed two lead guitar parts (John), piano (Paul), bass (Paul), percussion (Paul and John) and finally their vocals. The first Beatles song to be mixed solely in stereo – the birth of a new era – also brought another era to an end. Though it was far from the last time Lennon and McCartney worked together in the studio, it was their last major artistic collaboration.

OLD BROWN SHOE

GEORGE HARRISON

RECORDED 16, 18 APRIL 1969

Even when John Lennon was available to play on a Harrison song, an increasingly infrequent event by 1969, his instrumental contribution wasn't used in the final mix – his rhythm guitar losing its place to George's Hammond organ part. Otherwise, George's rocker was a four-man effort, thrown together with seemingly haphazard enthusiasm to create a suitable off-the-cuff flipside for 'The Ballad Of John And Yoko'. Harrison even allowed himself one of his loudest guitar solos on record as a rare moment of self-indulgence.

ACROSS THE UNIVERSE
JOHN LENNON/PAUL McCARTNEY
RECORDED 4, 8 FEBRUARY 1968, 2 OCTOBER 1969

For a song whose creation was so painless – Lennon woke in the night with the melody in his head, and the words waiting to flow out of his mind – 'Across The Universe' proved difficult to capture on tape. Ironically, the most perfect version of the song exists only on an EMI acetate, documenting the state of progress at the end of the first day's work. At that point, the song was punctuated by eerily beautiful bursts of backwards electric guitar, which were wiped from the tape at the start of Day Two.

That second session ended with the group uncertain where to go next. They'd already broken new ground by inviting two young fans, Lizzie Bravo and Gayleen Pease, in from the Abbey Road steps to add vocal harmonies; and Lennon himself contributed an exquisitely precise lead vocal. But he was still dissatisfied with the results. Plans to issue the track as a single were dropped, and the attempt to re-cut the song during the 'Let It Be' sessions failed.

Eventually, the track was made available to the World Wildlife Fund, for a 1969 charity LP called 'No One's Gonna Change Our World'. As the lead-off track, 'Across The Universe' was overdubbed with wildlife sounds by George Martin in October 1969. Six months later, another producer, Phil Spector, prepared his own mix of the song (see 'LET IT BE').

LET IT BE
JOHN LENNON/PAUL McCARTNEY
RECORDED 31 JANUARY, 30 APRIL 1969, 4 JANUARY 1970

This was the George Martin mix of the song, rather than what John Lennon called the "fruity" Phil Spector mix (see 'LET IT BE'). Spector heightened the percussion and chose a raucous Harrison guitar solo; for the group's final UK single, George Martin made more conservative choices.

YOU KNOW MY NAME (LOOK UP THE NUMBER)

JOHN LENNON/PAUL McCARTNEY

RECORDED 17 MAY, 7, 8 JUNE 1967, 30 APRIL, 26 NOVEMBER 1969

The Beatles' career as Britain's greatest singles band ended with this off-the-wall track, issued on the flipside of 'Let It Be'. It began life during the sessions for 'Magical Mystery Tour', with Brian Jones of The Rolling Stones playing saxophone, was left to one side for two years, then overdubbed during the recording of 'Abbey Road'. Once The Beatles' split was confirmed, towards the end of 1969, Lennon decided to rescue the track, and planned to issue it as a Plastic Ono Band single, alongside another Beatles off-cut, 'What's The News Mary Jane'. That plan was stymied, and so the song ended up as a Beatles recording after all.

"It's probably my favourite Beatles track," said Paul McCartney, "just because it's so insane. It was just so hilarious to put that record together." And the humour survives, from the deliberately over-the-top repetition of the title, to the Goons-like parade of vocal imitations that Lennon and McCartney unveiled for the last three minutes of the song. More than any other Beatles recording, it captures the sheer pleasure that was their lasting legacy to the world.

The Beatles
1962-1966 (The Red Album)

PARLOPHONE
BEACD 2511

1967-1970 (The Blue Album)

PARLOPHONE
BEACD 2512

In September of 1993, after much procrastination due apparently to The Beatles' own refusal to sanction their release, EMI finally issued the two Beatles' double albums of 'greatest hits' on CD. Universally known as the red and blue albums, their release caused no little controversy owing to Apple's insistence of their being produced as two double CDs – and priced accordingly – despite the fact that the two red albums lasted a total of only 62 minutes 46 seconds (and could therefore fit on to one CD). Critics were quick to point out that while the blue album ran over the limit for one CD (99.36), by shuffling the tracks around and deleting one from the blue album ('Octopus's Garden' perhaps?), the four CD package could easily have been issued as a two CD set at around £25 for the pair instead of around £50. EMI – and Paul McCartney via a spokesman – defended themselves against the critics as best they could but the general tone of the press coverage was that for the first time ever, The Beatles had been guilty of short-changing their fans. Nevertheless, the albums quickly ascended the charts and, of course, the music is wonderful.

Three sets of recordings taped before The Beatles' rise to fame have been issued on a variety of official, and unofficial, CDs over the last decade. Their release has often been surrounded by arguments over copyright, and their current status (bootleg or legal) still isn't clear. But unlike the bootleg releases of Beatles' live recordings, BBC sessions and studio out-takes, you will find CDs featuring this material on sale in record stores that pride themselves on their adherence to the law.

The Tony Sheridan Sessions

MY BONNIE (CHARLES PRATT)/**CRY FOR A SHADOW** (JOHN LENNON/GEORGE HARRISON)/**AIN'T SHE SWEET** (JACK YELLEN/MILTON AGER)/**WHY** (TONY SHERIDAN/BILL CROMPTON)/**TAKE OUT SOME INSURANCE FOR ME BABY (sometimes listed as IF YOU LOVE ME BABY)** (CHARLES SINGLETON/WALDENESE HALL)/**SWEET GEORGIA BROWN** (BEN BERNIE/MACEO PINKARD/KENNETH CASEY)/**THE SAINTS** (TRADITIONAL, ARRANGED TONY SHERIDAN)/**NOBODY'S CHILD** (MEL FOREE/CY COHEN)

The Beatles' first experience of a professional recording studio didn't turn out the way they'd imagined. Signed as backing group to London rocker Tony Sheridan during one of their first visits to Hamburg, they expected to be whisked straight to Polydor Records' German HQ for champagne and state-of-the-art technology. Instead, they wound up in a Hamburg school hall, taping eight tracks which have haunted them ever since.

The original deal, arranged by German producer and bandleader Bert Kaempfert, was for The Beatles to back Sheridan on a single, 'My Bonnie'/'The Saints'. That duly appeared as a single, credited to Tony Sheridan and The Beat Boys, in the summer of 1961. During the same sessions (or possibly as much as a year later, as the chronology of this period is still hazy), they taped six other tracks – four of them supporting Sheridan, two without his help. The latter were an instrumental, 'Cry For A Shadow', and John Lennon's first recorded lead vocal, 'Ain't She Sweet'.

These eight tracks, plus variations (there are two slightly different versions of 'My Bonnie', for instance, while Tony Sheridan re-recorded the lead vocal for 'Sweet Georgia Brown' in 1964) have appeared on countless LPs and now CDs since the mid-Sixties, often with Tony Sheridan's name relegated to the small print, and almost always alongside Sheridan record-ings which have no Beatles involvement. Some companies have dared to package the tracks with a sleeve showing a photo of the group after 1962, only for Apple to intervene with a fistful of writs. In the end, the eight songs are only of minor importance, particularly the Sheridan vocals, behind which the backing is so anonymous that it could have been anyone.

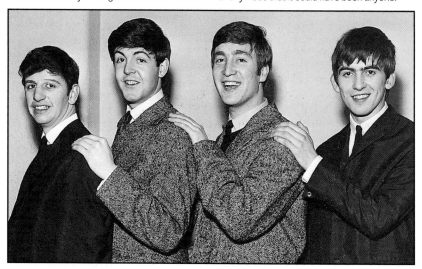

The DECCA Audition

BESAME MUCHO (CONSUELO VELASQUEZ/SELIG SHAFTEL)/**HELLO LITTLE GIRL** (JOHN LENNON/PAUL MCCARTNEY)/**THE SHEIK OF ARABY** (HARRY SMITH/TED SNYDER/FRANCES WHEELER)/**SEPTEMBER IN THE RAIN** (AL DUBIN/HARRY WARREN)/**THREE COOL CATS** (JERRY LEIBER/MIKE STOLLER)/**LOVE OF THE LOVED** (JOHN LENNON/PAUL MCCARTNEY)/**MEMPHIS, TENNESSEE** (CHUCK BERRY)/**TILL THERE WAS YOU** (MEREDITH WILLSON)/**CRYING, WAITING, HOPING** (BUDDY HOLLY)/**LIKE DREAMERS DO** (JOHN LENNON/PAUL MCCARTNEY)/**MONEY** (BERRY GORDY/JANIE BRADFORD)/**SEARCHIN'** (JERRY LEIBER/MIKE STOLLER)/**SURE TO FALL** (CARL PERKINS/WILLIAM CANTRELL/QUINTON CLAUNCH)/**TO KNOW HER IS TO LOVE HER** (PHIL SPECTOR)/**TAKE GOOD CARE OF MY BABY** (GERRY GOFFIN/CAROLE KING)

On January 1, 1962, The Beatles celebrated New Year by recording 15 songs for Decca A&R man Mike Smith at the label's West Hampstead studios. It was their first encounter with the London record industry, and it ended in disappointment, when Decca (in the person of the much-maligned Dick Rowe, under advice from Smith) chose instead to sign another of the day's auditionees, Brian Poole & The Tremeloes, because they came from Dagenham rather than Liverpool and would therefore have a shorter distance to travel to recording sessions.

Listening to the contents of the tape, which first surfaced on bootleg in the late Seventies, it was easy to see why The Beatles didn't become Decca recording artists. They sound appallingly stilted and ill-at-ease; McCartney over-sings every lead vocal, while Lennon is subdued; Pete Best's drumming is little more than basic; and only George Harrison comes through the audition with his reputation intact.

The historical value of the tape was enor-mous, of course. Rumour had it that Decca executives pulled it out of the vault every Christmas and drowned their sorrows while they listened to it one more time, trying to dis-cover how they missed out on the world's best-selling pop group. Ownership of the tape was open to question, however, and in 1982 the US label Backstage Records took the plunge. With the backing of Pete Best, they issued ten of the audition tracks on an 'official'

LP set. The more established Audio-Fidelity label followed suit a few months later, upping the contents to 12 songs – but omitting the three Lennon/McCartney compositions, in the hope of avoiding legal tangles. For the next few years, these 12 tracks appeared on countless LPs and CDs, before the lawyers took control. No-one still seems sure who owns the rights to the tracks, but no-one has dared to reissue them since the late 80s, either.

Live at the Star Club, Hamburg

I SAW HER STANDING THERE (JOHN LENNON/PAUL MCCARTNEY)/I'M GONNA SIT RIGHT DOWN AND CRY (OVER YOU) (JOE THOMAS/HOWARD BIGGS)/ROLL OVER BEETHOVEN (CHUCK BERRY)/THE HIPPY HIPPY SHAKE (CHAN ROMERO)/SWEET LITTLE SIXTEEN (CHUCK BERRY)/LEND ME YOUR COMB (KAY TWOMEY/FRED WISE/BEN WEISMAN)/YOUR FEET'S TOO BIG (ADA BENSON/FRED FISHER)/WHERE HAVE YOU BEEN ALL MY LIFE? (BARRY MANN/CYNTHIA WEIL)/TWIST AND SHOUT (BERT RUSSELL/PHIL MEDLEY)/MR. MOONLIGHT (ROY LEE JOHNSON)/A TASTE OF HONEY (RIC MARLOW/BOBBY SCOTT)/BESAME MUCHO (CONSUELO VELASQUEZ/SELIG SHAFTEL)/REMINISCING (KING CURTIS)/TILL THERE WAS YOU (MEREDITH WILLSON)/EVERYBODY'S TRYING TO BE MY BABY (CARL PERKINS)/KANSAS CITY; HEY HEY HEY HEY (JERRY LEIBER/MIKE STOLLER; RICHARD PENNIMAN)/NOTHIN' SHAKIN' (BUT THE LEAVES ON THE TREE) (CIRINO COLACRAI/EDDIE FONTAINE/DIANNE LAMPERT/JACK CLEVELAND)/TO KNOW HER IS TO LOVE HER (PHIL SPECTOR)/LITTLE QUEENIE (CHUCK BERRY)/FALLING IN LOVE AGAIN (SAMMY LERNER/FREDERICK HOLLANDER)/SHEILA (TOMMY ROE)/BE-BOP-A-LULA (GENE VINCENT/TEX DAVIS)/HALLELUJAH I LOVE HER SO (RAY CHARLES)/ASK ME WHY (JOHN LENNON/PAUL MCCARTNEY)/RED SAILS IN THE SUNSET (JIMMY KENNEDY/WILL GROSZ)/MATCHBOX (CARL PERKINS)/I'M TALKIN' 'BOUT YOU (CHUCK BERRY)/I WISH I COULD SHIMMY LIKE MY SISTER KATE (PIRON)/LONG TALL SALLY (RICHARD PENNIMAN/ENOTRIS JOHNSON/ROBERT BLACKWELL)/I REMEMBER YOU (JOHNNY MERCER/VICTOR SCHERTZINGER)

John Lennon: "We were performers and what we generated was fantastic. We played straight rock, and there was nobody to touch us in Britain. Brian put us in suits and all that, and we made it very, very big. But we sold out. We always missed the club dates because that's when we were playing music.

Paul McCartney: "In Hamburg, we'd work eight hours a day, while most bands never worked that hard. So we had developed our act, and by the time we came to America, we had all that worked out. When we started off in Hamburg, we had no audience, so we had to work our asses off to get people in. People would appear at the door of the club while we were on stage and there would be nobody at the tables. We used to try to get them in to sell beer. The minute we saw them, we'd just rock out, and we'd find we'd got three of them in. We were like fairground barkers. We eventually sold the club out, which is when we realised it was going to get really big."

The appearance in 1977 of 30 songs recorded during the final week of The Beatles' life as a club band in Hamburg, Germany, gave the rest of the world its first chance to hear the music behind the legend. Many people were disappointed: The Beatles sounded less like "fairground barkers" than bored, overworked money-slaves – which is exactly what they were, as they plodded through their last exhausting German shows, knowing the prospect of stardom awaited them at home in Britain.

Even under these less than promising circumstances, though, the Star-Club tapes do capture the manic humour and rock'n'roll prowess of the pre-fame Beatles. But those qualities are mostly buried in the muddiness of the sound, which is the best that can be achieved from the impromptu amateur source-tape.

That was made by Liverpudlian engineer Adrian Barber, who went on to produce the MC5 and The Velvet Underground in New York many years later. Via a series of pub encounters, the raw tape ended up with original Beatles manager Allan Williams. He offered it to Brian Epstein, who turned it down; a decade later, he played it to George and Ringo at Apple, who loved what they heard, but still didn't come up with a deal.

Eventually, Williams took the tape to Lingasong Records in London, who cleaned it up and readied it for release. Apple belatedly tried to prevent the release, but failed. The tracks have since been issued on a variety of LPs and CDs, often with completely misleading credits, and their current legal status is uncertain. Strangely, the one company who had a perfect right to stop the release, but seem to have made no attempt to do so, was EMI: when it was recorded, on December 31, 1962, The Beatles were under exclusive contract with its Parlophone subsidiary. Lingasong cleverly sidestepped this question by claiming that the tape pre-dated the signing of the deal, something which the evidence of the tape itself proved to be false.

Track Listing

A Day In The Life 63

A Hard Day's Night 18

A Taste Of Honey...6, 131

Across The Universe.......................................103, 123

Act Naturally...36

Ain't She Sweet 127

All I've Got To Do 10

All My Loving 10

All Together Now 88

All You Need Is Love 71, 89

And I Love Her...20

And Your Bird Can Sing 53

Anna (Go To Him)...3

Another Girl...35

Any Time At All 21

Ask Me Why 4, 131

Baby It's You 6

Baby You're A Rich Man 71

Baby's In Black 27

Back In The USSR 75

Bad Boy 115

Be-Bop-A-Lula 131

Because 96

Being For The Benefit Of Mr Kite 61

Besame Mucho...129, 131

Birthday 80

Blackbird 78

Blue Album 1967-1970 125

Blue Jay Way 67

Boys 3

Can't Buy Me Love 21

Carry That Weight 98

Chains 3

Come Together 92

Cry Baby Cry..84

Cry For A Shadow 127

Crying, Waiting, Hoping...129

Day Tripper...117

Dear Prudence 75

Devil In Her Heart 14

Dig A Pony 103

Dig It...104

Dizzy Miss Lizzy 39

Do You Want To Know A Secret?................................6

Doctor Robert 54

Don't Bother Me 11

Don't Let Me Down 121

Don't Pass Me By 79

Drive My Car 42
Eight Days A Week 29
Eleanor Rigby 50
Every Little Thing 30
Everybody's Got Something
  To Hide Except Me And My Monkey 81
Everybody's Trying To Be My Baby 31, 131
Falling In Love Again 131
Fixing A Hole 60
Flying 67
For No One 54
For You Blue 106
From Me To You 109
Get Back 107, 121
Getting Better 60
Girl 45
Glass Onion 76
Golden Slumbers 98
Good Day Sunshine 53
Good Morning, Good Morning 62
Good Night 85
Got To Get You Into My Life 55
Hallelujah I Love Her So 131
Happiness Is A Warm Gun 77
Hello Goodbye 68
Hello Little Girl 129
Help! 34

Helter Skelter 82
Her Majesty 99
Here Comes The Sun 96
Here, There And Everywhere 51
Hey Bulldog 88
Hey, Hey, Hey, Hey 28, 131
Hey Jude 119
Hold Me Tight 13
Honey Don't 29
Honey Pie 84
I Am The Walrus 68
I Call Your Name 112
I Don't Want To Spoil The Party 30
I Feel Fine 114
I Me Mine 104
I Need You 35
I Remember You 131
I Saw Her Standing There 2, 131
I Should Have Known Better 19
I Wanna Be Your Man 14
I Want To Hold Your Hand 111
I Want To Tell You 54
I Want You (She's So Heavy) 94
I Will 80
I Wish I Could Shimmy Like My Sister Kate 131
I'll Be Back 23
I'll Cry Instead 22

I'll Follow The Sun..28
I'll Get You...111
I'm A Loser..26
I'm Down..115
I'm Gonna Sit Right Down And Cry Over You...131
I'm Happy Just To Dance With You...................19
I'm Looking Through You....................................46
I'm Only Sleeping..51
I'm So Tired...78
I'm Talkin' 'Bout You...131
I've Got A Feeling...105
I've Just Seen A Face..38
If I Fell...19
If I Needed Someone..47
If You Love Me Baby...127
In My Life...46
It Won't Be Long..10
It's All Too Much..89
It's Only Love...36
Julia...80
Kansas City..28, 131
Komm, Gib Mir Deine Hand.............................112
Lady Madonna..119
Lend Me Your Comb...131
Let It Be 24, 105, 123
Like Dreamers Do...129
Little Child..12

Little Queenie..131
Long Long Long..83
Long Tall Sally 112, 131
Love Me Do 5, 109
Love Of The Loved...129
Love You To...51
Lovely Rita...62
Lucy In The Sky With Diamonds........................59
Maggie Mae...105
Magical Mystery Tour...66
Martha My Dear...78
Matchbox...114, 131
Maxwell's Silver Hammer...................................93
Mean Mr Mustard...97
Memphis Tennessee...129
Michelle...45
Misery 2
Money (That's What I Want) 14, 129
Mother Nature's Son..81
Mr. Moonlight...28, 131
My Bonnie...127
No Reply..26
Nobody's Child...127
Norwegian Wood..42
Not A Second Time...14
Nothing' Shakin' (But The Leaves On the Tree).131
Nowhere Man...43

Ob-La-Di, Ob-La-Da 76
Octopus's Garden...94
Oh! Darling 94
Old Brown Shoe...122
One After 909 106
Only A Northern Song......................................88
P.S. I Love You...5
Paperback Writer 118
Penny Lane 69
Piggies 78
Please Mr. Postman 12
Please Please Me...4
Polythene Pam 97
Rain..118
Red Album 1962-1966......................................125
Red Sails In The Sunset 131
Reminiscing..131
Revolution 120
Revolution 1 83
Revolution 9 85
Rock And Roll Music 27
Rocky Raccoon 79
Roll Over Beethoven 13, 131
Run For Your Life 47
Savoy Truffle 84
Searchin' 129
September In The Rain 129

Sexy Sadie 82
Sgt. Pepper's Lonely Hearts Club Band............59
Sgt. Pepper's Lonely Hearts Club Band (Reprise).62
She Came In Through The Bathroom Window ...97
She Loves You...110
She Said She Said 53
She's A Woman 114
She's Leaving Home 60
Sheila 131
Sie Liebt Dich 112
Slow Down...113
Something...93
Strawberry Fields Forever 69
Sun King...97
Sure To Fall 129
Sweet Georgia Brown.......................................127
Sweet Little Sixteen 131
Take Good Care Of My Baby.............................129
Take Out Some Insurance For Me Baby 127
Taxman..50
Tell Me What You See 38
Tell Me Why 21
Thank You Girl...110
The Ballad Of John And Yoko 122
The Continuing Story Of Bungalow Bill............77
The End...99
The Fool On The Hill 66

The Hippy Hippy Shake 131
The Inner Light 119
The Long And Winding Road 106
The Night Before 34
The Saints 127
The Sheik Of Araby 129
The Word 45
There's A Place 7
Things We Said Today.....................................22
Think For Yourself 43
This Boy 111
Three Cool Cats 129
Ticket To Ride 36
Till There Was You 12, 129, 131
To Know Her Is To Love Her 129, 131
Tomorrow Never Knows 55
Twist And Shout...............................7, 131
Two Of Us 103
Wait...46
We Can Work It Out..117
What Goes On? 45
What You're Doing..31
When I Get Home 23
When I'm Sixty-Four..62
Where Have You Been All My Life 131
While My Guitar Gently Weeps.........................77
Why..127

Why Don't We Do It In The Road? 79
Wild Honey Pie...76
With A Little Help From My Friends...................59
Within You Without You....................................61
Words Of Love..29
Yellow Submarine 52, 88
Yer Blues..81
Yes It Is 115
Yesterday..38
You Can't Do That...23
You Know My Name (Look Up The Number)...124
You Like Me Too Much 38
You Never Give Me Your Money 96
You Won't See Me 43
Your Feet's Too Big 131
You're Gonna Lose That Girl............................36
You've Got To Hide Your Love Away 35
You Really Got A Hold On Me...........................14
Your Mother Should Know 67

3/95 (19806